HAPPY HEALING

What Would You Do If
It Happened to You?

Debbie Betesh

ISBN: 978-1-66783-071-1 (Print)
ISBN: 978-1-66783-072-8 (eBook)

TABLE OF CONTENTS

For Marcelle, Linda, and Abe

Channeling My Red Aura:

Auras are the energy fields humans emit. Me? I'm a red aura kind of gal. I've always had this out-of-the-box attitude—thinking big, living large, and catapulting myself completely into everything with tremendous chutzpah to boast. My persistence is due to my red aura. It gives me amazing champion forces of zeal, vitality, and ferocity. My energy makes my life extraordinary. I live, breathe, and feel all this color has to offer me. I risk more than others think is wise and seek success at any cost. It's in my blood to have this outlook on life. I've learned from experience to taper my powerful red aura and enable it to influence my unique ways of problem solving and desire to always be on the move. My cravings for constant motion and physical activity were satiated with daily weight training and bodybuilding activities. My omnipotence made me feel like I could hold the weight of the world on my shoulders like the Greek god Atlas.

Everything appeared to be going well, or so I thought. I was making great strides in life and perfected my strength training exercises. If you saw me back at my bodybuilding prime, I'd bet you'd be able to see the red aura emitting from my body without the help of an aura-detecting camera! I was strong, passionate, and dedicated to all aspects of my life. Who knew my gig could be up and it could all come tumbling down in a sudden moment? I told myself that even Atlas's back gets tired sometimes. I was about to undergo a step-by-step transformation in which my determination and marvelous mentality would be the keys to my success!

One day in 2009, I wasn't feeling like my normal red aura self. I sensed death breathing down my neck. I was suddenly drowning in pain on the floor. I felt my aura take on blackened hues. It was like my physical body was no longer on the electromagnetic spectrum. How did I get there and how did I lose control of my body? I remembered coming from work, entering the New York Sports Club, and doing my intense regimen on the leg press for 10 sets, shooting for 50 reps, followed by push-ups in between each set. I knew so many onlookers at the gym envied my level of fitness and how it felt to be so robust and resilient. But now, I was flat on the floor.

The searing pain reentered my consciousness. I had reached my own life's apocalypse and started to hyperventilate. Immobile, frozen with neck and back pain, I saw my life flash before my eyes. I couldn't speak or move. The pain consumed me. It felt like death was swallowing me whole and I was forced into fight-or-flight. Since I have a red aura, I'm a survival-oriented situation solver. I'm equipped to take out that battle armor and fight. The struggle was real. I fought for my life and would not let this catastrophe define me. With my power to push through the pain and get up from the floor, I realized I had the strength to be in the driver's seat of recovery.

What would you do if this happened to you?

CHAPTER 1:

Looking Out of the Box

When my red aura started to fade from my injuries, it was time to take immediate action, channel my inner strength, and bring the color back to its familial hue. From that point, I embarked on an odyssey to resurrect my supreme self. Welcome to *Happy Healing*, my recovery story of bravery, faith, and triumph. Overcoming my challenges required great amounts of strength and love. I overcame my issues and am no longer a victim. I am a victor. Here's what I looked like in my bodybuilding prime, just before my accident:

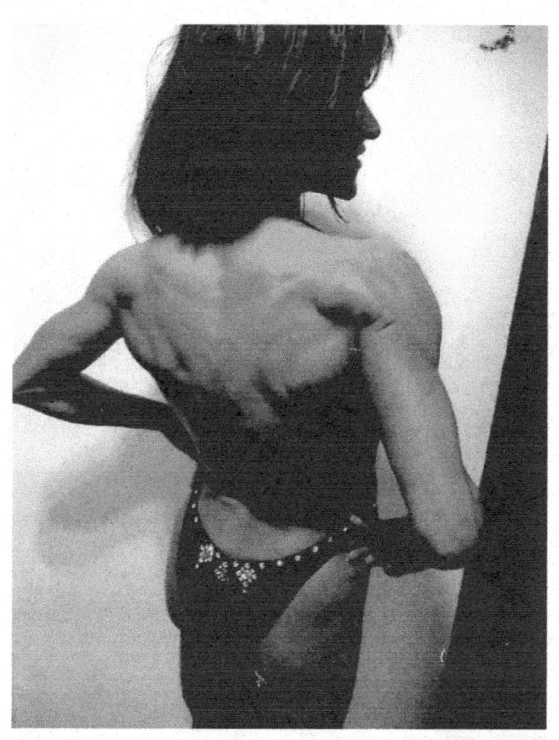

I participated in the National Physique Committee's Eastern USA Bodybuilding Competition in the women's physique category. During my bodybuilding career from 2000-2009, I worked out twice daily, ate protein every three hours during training days, and drank lots of water to flush my body. Can you believe how ripped I was? It's even hard for me to remember how I once looked like this and strained my body over the course of nine years to the umpteenth degree to reach this level of fitness. I suffered from several serious medical issues because of the pressure I put on my body: The pain I felt stemmed from physical issues I couldn't simply shrug off my shoulders, literally and physically.

I made myself into a bodybuilder with dedication. After my accident, I used this same determination to heal myself. If I told you that I cured myself without traditional methods, like painkillers or surgery, you'd probably think I'm insane. Well, it's not so wild at all because I am living proof that it worked. There is a strategic method behind my unconventional madness. And now, I am stronger than ever. This is my beautiful life and I love every minute of it. The alternative methods I found to recuperate launched my path of *Happy Healing*. I embraced the universe's power on the road to recovery. My healing goals included loosening my body once I started to feel better. I even took up dancing and am still in the process of transforming my former bodybuilder-self into a fluid dancer as part of this journey. Blissful healing is ongoing! As each new day arrives, I am still making progress. I'm freer, becoming more flexible, and feeling more alive. I am stronger than ever before in many different ways — all without having to hit the gym to weightlift. You'd better believe it!

I have chosen to write this book to inspire you about healing. I want you to question modern medicine and explore all options when recovering from an injury and I want you to become re-inspired about life. I hope to encourage you to listen to your body while finding what works best for you. I want you to open your mind to alternative healing options just like I have opened mine.

As a native New Yorker, I like when things are completed speedily in a "New York" minute. I tend to be proactive, rather than reactive, seeking techniques that will work in the fastest and most effective ways. Unfortunately, the healing process is not something that occurs overnight. With my exceptional way of thinking, I was able devise a natural recovery plan for my injured state.

Healing is a labor of love. It is also like having another job—something that you truly have to work at to reap the benefits and learn in the process by trial and error. All good things, like healing, take time. To me, trying different curative treatments was like dating: taking each one seriously, playing the field until I found the right fit, and knowing that my life would change forever. Because my life was in jeopardy from the injuries, the daunting thought of healing seemed bigger than life itself.

I feel that my healing process is an achievement that I can add to my star-studded resume, which currently includes the awe-inspiring titles of Mom, Bodybuilder, Real Estate Guru, Corporate Account Professional at a garbage service company (which is more like a hobby of mine), Life Insurance Agent Extraordinaire, Dancer, and Social Activist with the Precious Child Act (to educate New York State's children about sexual abuse). So, I suppose I should start at the very beginning of how I'm still here, standing proudly, strutting stronger, and dancing through life—literally and figuratively.

I firmly believe the universe works in your favor. I think I have pronoia, which is the idea that the universe is good-giving and here to help me along the way. My pronoia, combined with my strong faith and positive outlook on life, enabled me to have my wishes granted. When I think differently, I keep all these factors in mind. I am convinced that the world is scheming goodness to disperse around. "If you ask, you shall receive" is a motto I've lived by, and it has driven me to succeed in various areas of my life, including healing. I always experience these unbelievable moments that you cannot even make up!

One of the first times I had a "pinch me" moment was in May 1997. Rewind! Let's take a time warp to the scene of the event: I was driving home from the dentist at dusk. I was thinking about future steps I should take with my career. As I drove into the Brooklyn Battery Tunnel, I contemplated my options. "Debbie, what should I do? I need to make a decision fast. I need answers right now! It shouldn't be this hard to make a decision. It is really simple." My internal dialogue questioned what career path I should take. I also wanted to do what made me happy. Because I specialized in wearing many hats and needed to always be hands-on in many ventures at once, I didn't know if I should go into real estate, life insurance, or both. My real estate and life insurance licenses were both going to expire that September. I had to act fast on this urgent matter and needed to know which to renew!

During the drive, I noticed how the sky looked exceptionally majestic. The sunset-streaked sky intertwined its blue and red hues. It was one of the best sunsets I had ever seen. Divine intervention was about to occur and I was about to have a revelation.

Being the full supporter of my children, I needed to care for them while taking the next step in my career. My kids were, and still are, my life. (Mom-hood is absolutely my favorite job thus far, of course!)

During my heavy duty thinking session in the car, I adhered to my principles, concentrated on my red aura's energy, and relied on my vigorous strength. I realized that I could do anything with my willpower. I went back to basics and prayed to Hashem (God) for a sign. Because I am an extremely spiritual person, I needed a clue that would provide me the answer I was looking for. I was frantic.

When I drove out of the tunnel, a white van cut me off with the license plate that read "LIFE INS." I screamed in delight because I could not believe my eyes. I said, "Am I seeing things?" But it was real! It was so incredible! It felt like I was dreaming. This divine sign explicitly told me to further my career in life insurance. I called my rabbi Dweck from Deal, New Jersey, and told him about the sign I just saw. He inquired, "So, Debbie, what are ya' going to do?" I was enlightened! I told my rabbi how I planned to renew my life insurance license and jump headfirst into the industry. Later on, I even decided to pursue real estate as well to have the best of both worlds because I liked staying busy. This event is proof of how the method of positive thinking, asking, and receiving works. These techniques and tools would especially come in handy later in my life. Also, understanding how to take everything back to its simplest means became important too.

Flash forward to the year 2009: I was living in Brooklyn in a lovely three-story brick house that I purchased 19 years prior. From the loft bedroom in the attic to the porch that wrapped around the front, I loved that place. It held the distinctive memories of raising my three kids. At the time, my eldest daughter lived in California while my son and younger daughter still lived with me. My kids were in their 20s and had jam-packed school and work schedules. We perfected our daily routines and loved spending time together.

The morning of my accident was just like any other morning. I woke up and lifted the shades to watch the sunrise. Birds chirped from the trees outside my windows and the only noises heard on the streets were school buses chugging by. It reminded me of the old days when I was rushing to get my kids to school. But since they were older and slept through the a.m. hours, my mornings were kick-started with a nice workout. For the next forty minutes, I had an energizing session on the elliptical set to The Rolling Stones' greatest hits. I blasted the music and loved how I knew every tune. After my shower, I headed to the kitchen to make a chocolate peanut butter protein drink, my favorite reward and recovery drink after exercising. Without this pre-work routine, my day would seem incomplete. This routine was so awesome!

With a full stomach and a clear head, I was pumped to start another day at work. Let me give you a quick background of my work—I've always had interesting jobs. In 2007, I was hands-on at my family's real estate business, In 2008, I wanted to try something different and left to work for an independent real estate agency. It was a great experience, but after a year and a half, I busted out of there and went back to the family office.

Still to this day, I enjoy sealing the deal and embracing the rush of the real estate industry. It's been a learning process and I have earned my superstar status in my field. Real estate is in my blood, as this company has been a part of my family for most of my life. If that job wasn't enough, I also worked, and still work, for Royal Waste Services where I have been selling containers to construction sites since 2008. Sure, classifying me as an overachiever would be correct. I absolutely love working with people, talking to clients, and giving them what they're looking for. All my jobs are great!

My daily workday journey started with taking the super-crowded B train into Manhattan. Thirty minutes later, I started my daily vice presidential real estate duties or at Royal Waste Removal Services. This day in particular, in 2009, I was wearing my real estate hat. I had so much energy. I felt like I could rotate the Earth, move mountains, and be home in time for dinner. It was a typical busy day at the office—tons of paperwork, demanding clients, and a long list of appointments. I loved the craziness, the demanding schedule, and the hard work. Because I enjoy it so tremendously, I work these jobs still to this day. I work hard and play even harder.

When 5:00 p.m. rolled around, I took the train back to Brooklyn, enthusiastically grabbed my gym bag, and was ready for my second workout of the day at New York Sports Club. With my inner Olympian strength, I walked in, waved to the regulars, and changed my clothes in preparation for training. I was extraordinarily passionate about my training sessions and I took them very seriously. You name any intense workout, I bet I could have done it. Push-ups? Absolutely! I'd do about 20 in a minute! Dead lifting? You bet! Pull-ups, yeah, they were the most difficult, but I got through them. My trainer used to help me do the pull-ups and picked up my body to help me out. I loved the challenge.

The day of the incident, I headed for the leg press, pushed 45 pounds on each side of the bar with my goal of 50 reps. Next, I hit the floor for one round of push-ups, then headed back to the leg press for another intense round, aiming for 10 sets of my entire circuit. I had to maintain my muscular physique. Awe-stricken people gathered around in wonder to watch the incredible one-woman spectacle. I was actually a superwoman!

Because I loved going to the gym so much, I ignored the pain I was having. I thought I was having a great time at the gym that day and thought that the discomfort was just muscular fatigue. Suddenly, the pain got worse. It shot through my shoulder and raced up my neck. It felt like someone had stabbed me from behind! I was paralyzed with pain.

I can recall the exact timing of my accident. I was in the midst of doing my set of push-ups when I pushed downward, and fell flat on the floor. The last thing I remember was saying to myself, "Just one more round of push-ups, just one more round of push-ups. You can do it!" And then all I could see was the floor. The fellow gym-goers gathered closer and watched as I fell. They later informed me that I fell slowly and then all at once, like a tree falling in the wilderness. As I was going down, my life flashed before my eyes, and then I blacked out.

Since I am in-tune with my spirituality, times like these caused me to draw upon the strength tarot card that represents my essence and date of birth. I draw upon my strength to successfully complete tasks. Like the lion on the tarot card, I emitted prideful roars and was able to regain my wits about me. My friend once told me I have a fighting spirit. And I do. Because I am a champion, I redeemed consciousness, gathered stamina, and remembered how strong I was.

"Are you okay?" people yelled from the sidelines. "Should we call the ambulance?" "Do you need medical attention?" "Can you walk?"

Concerned gym buddies bombarded me. I opened my eyes, slowly stood up like a boxer regaining her strength from being pummeled down to the ground during a match, and rose from the ground. I assured everyone that I was okay. All I could think about was getting home to my kids, and I needed to leave to lie down. That strength enabled me to walk away from the gym, get in the car, head home, and collapse. I was still in agony.

How did I make it and drive home by myself? My strength! It was simply a case of "mind over matter." I concentrated on the situation at hand, sparked by my body's release of adrenaline. I kept remembering how strong I was and I wished that the pain would subside. On my ride home, the simplest task of sitting upright in the car was unbearable!

I arrived home and felt like I had been dragged through the Midtown Tunnel and run over by three Mack trucks. I collapsed in a heap on my bed and tried to rest, hoping this was all just a bad dream. I thought I would get up the next day and hop right back on my elliptical, just like I did every morning.

My mishap wasn't a dream. It was a living, breathing nightmare. The next morning, I could barely walk. I could hardly stand, clothe myself, and hop in a cab to see my doctor. After waiting for what seemed like an eternity, I received a quick examination from my doctor, and he prescribed some pain medication. I was willing to do anything to make the pain subside, so I had no choice but to take the pills.

Next was the MRI. I arrived in the sterile room and it looked like a walk-in freezer. The scanner was basically a huge, futuristic-looking contraption from a science fiction movie. I had to lie down on a table and was put inside a massive device by the technician who assured the scan would be painless. Despite the warning, it was so painful! I was really concerned about the harsh reality of my situation. I was now a patient—another person suffering from a condition due to terrible circumstances. Just like that, everything was at risk. I was nervous about what the unknown held. How would I provide for my kids, continue my career, and proceed with my life?

The MRI results came back quickly, showing three herniated discs: one between the fourth and fifth vertebrae; a second between the fifth and sixth vertebrae; and a third between the sixth and seventh vertebrae. With the second spot, the thick membrane surrounding the spinal cord was deformed. The nerves in the second and third locations were compressed on both sides of the spine, the cause of my excruciating pain. I was informed that the official diagnosis was a mild bilateral neural foraminal narrowing, an ailment that affects the spinal cord and all connecting nerves. Such problems occur when the foramen, or spaces in the bones, become narrow. When the nerves are compressed, pain is felt. These were some serious injuries. If mistreated, I could be permanently damaged for the rest of my life.

I was shocked with these results because I never expected this to happen. I thought I was doing the best for my body by constantly working out. I presumed I was in tip-top shape. I always knew that when the body is stagnant, disease occurs. So I put myself in perpetual motion. I had to remind myself to stay strong and think positively despite the circumstances.

Here I was in excruciating pain with three herniated discs in my neck, feeling stunned, frustrated, and frightened. Any injury to the spine, especially in the neck area, is cause for concern. I didn't know exactly what this would mean for me. While all these thoughts and feelings were swimming around in my head, my doctor gave me choices: first pain medication, then cortisone shots, then physical therapy, and lastly surgery. I wanted to avoid surgery. I got the prescription filled and started a new type of "normal" life.

Much to my dismay, my daily routine was disrupted. Instead of getting up in the morning and drawing back the blinds, I popped a pill in bed and waited twenty minutes for it to kick in. There was no jaunt on the elliptical, no sing-along to The Rolling Stones, no tasty protein shake, and no seamless trip to work. Instead, I dragged myself to the shower, got dressed in pain, and made a simple breakfast. Instead of my gym bag, I secured my neck brace and fastened it tightly for the subway ride. With the neck gear, I looked like a Martian all set to blast off into space. Every twist, turn, and bump of the train ran up my spine, hitting those herniated discs. It felt like someone was taking a hammer to my back's discs during the day. The pills did not fully mask the pain. In the office, I wasn't zipping around. I no longer felt energized, like I could lift the world, and my red aura was abnormally dull. It took me longer to get paperwork done and I sent colleagues to appointments. I just sat at my desk, swallowed more pills, and tried to get through my day. I longed to have my old life back. I missed my former self, the old Debra.

At the end of the day, I could not simply grab my gym bag and head to the sports club. My whole world was pain. It took over my life and I could not do any of my regular activities. I went straight home, found the nearest chair, and collapsed in a pain-fueled state of fatigue. As my condition progressed, I still devoted time to my kids, but not as much as I was accustomed to. My kids did not come home to a clean house and a home-cooked meal. I had to watch as they ordered out and did their own version of tidying up the place. I felt like I was failing my kids. The pain kept me home from many parties and family events. My son couldn't come and train with me at the gym because I no longer went. Shabbat dinners on Friday nights were never really the same either; my body was not up for fun or extreme movement of any kind. The most painful thing was that it even hurt to laugh. If I did manage to get myself out of the house, the neck brace was a major eyesore. I remember covering it up with a bedazzled, crystal sock for New Year's Eve so I could look somewhat normal.

I probably should have stayed home from work to recover, but my energetic attitude and strength would not allow me to just sit around. It was not in my personality to stay on the sidelines of the situation and sulk around the house. I was strong enough to handle recovery and work at the same time. By taking the medication, I could numb the pain and support my family. I had commitments to fulfill and pain to fix.

Meanwhile, my doctors recommended cortisone shots and physical therapy. I knew these solutions couldn't completely stop the constant pain. It was becoming obvious that the herniated discs would need extensive medical treatment. All of this seemed far off in the future. I dealt with the pain to start my mornings without trouble and get through the day without pain. My only relief came from the small brown bottle of Percocet that the doctors prescribed.

In the beginning, one pill was enough to numb my aching neck and my heart. The world became so small—only large enough for my pain and pills. There was not enough space for energy, excitement, or even good digestion. My stomach was all tied up in knots. Soon, one pill wasn't enough and I started taking two every couple of hours. The prescription drugs were all I had. I became dependent on them. I found myself always reaching for a pain pill. I was addicted, a victim of pills. Something needed to be done.

I complained to my doctors and told them the Percocet was practically useless. I said I needed something better or I wouldn't be able to function in everyday life. They strongly advised me to have the surgery. But in my mind, surgery was too scary. There were three displaced bones in my neck and no way to convince me that a discectomy, the surgical removal of the herniated discs, was a routine procedure. Undergoing any type of surgery is risky, especially with my condition. After surgery, I could need more surgeries and suffer damage to the spinal column. What happened if surgical complications paralyzed me? I couldn't even think about these risks.

What could I do now so I could work every day and complete everything that needed to get done? The only solution the doctors provided came in the form of additional painkillers. This time around I was given OxyContin, an upgrade from Percocet. I took an 80 mg pill twice a day. The side effects were almost as worse as the pain I experienced. My injuries were getting more painful, and other bodily issues developed. Because I was so strong, I ignored the original pain and overexerted myself through strength and muscle training. The neck injury was followed by a back injury, problems arose with my feet, and I had high blood pressure that forced me to face many trials and tribulations. Talk about a tough pill to swallow.

I always knew I needed to seek natural methods of healing, but I wanted to try the medicated route for immediate relief to tame the pain. And since the root of pain was not truly being healed anyway, I needed to seek alternative ways to get back on track. I'd always been in favor of holistic options like juicing, smoothies, cleansing, and consciously making proper dietary choices. I also had received frequent medical massages since 1991 from my family friend Ray Pergola, and they worked wonders for muscular pain. I figured holistic remedies could not hurt!

Because natural treatments had helped me in the past, I now had nothing to lose. Straying from medical norms like surgery and medication helped me find solutions to my problems. I needed to find a happy way of healing that suited me!

Natural healing does not occur inside the rigid constraints of ordinary healing. In order to successfully set yourself on track for a full recovery, you must do what you feel is best for your body. At this point, I asked to receive a sign that would point me to the proper natural treatment for my body. My wishes were about to be answered without any further pill popping. I was about to embark on a lifelong bud-like course of blossoming.

Although it has been a long journey, I am grateful that I followed my gut instincts through my special healing process. And this expedition for wellness is ongoing! Sometimes I look back at certain chapters in my life and wonder how I could have possibly made it through. I owe it all to my strength, spirituality, perseverance, and robust nature. I know I'm not alone because everyone faces adversities from time to time. Such setbacks come with the territory of being human. They can pave enduring passages and create stories to help others. Our existence is defined by the challenges we face and overcome. The universe ultimately gives us what we can handle.

Now at 58 years old, I feel like I'm aging backward. Currently, I am happy, healthy, and feel like a 40-year-old. I am truly grateful for what the universe has given me, and I was fortunate to look outside of the box to discover natural healing. My belief in a higher power, confident outlook on life, and stick-to-itiveness have served me well. Some people just settle for the current situation and say the cards they were dealt are set in stone. Not I! I had to be proactive. Instead of doing what the doctors suggested, I sought more wholesome and alternative ways to heal. Doing so changed my life's essence. Movement, breathing, and simplicity were soon revealed as the answers to my pain. I learned that I needed to heal with an open mind.

If you say what you mean and mean what you say, everything will happen in just that way. Power of the word is one of greatest things in the universe. Always be sure to express your intentions and be careful what you wish for. It's necessary to announce what you want to happen to take control of your future because what you put out to the cosmos you will receive right back. Articulate your intent in all aspects of your life. I decided early on that I would heal myself and would make a full recovery. I advantageously used affirmations to motivate myself on my healing journey. Each day, I'd tell myself, "Debbie, you will make a full recovery! Everything will get better! Keep heading down the healing path!" With my daily positive declamations, I convinced myself that I would fully heal and I honored my body. A study was once done in which two separate cups of rice were put on a countertop. The person told one cup of rice, "I love you" everyday. The other cup was told, "I hate you." Over a period of time, the "loved" rice looked better while the "hated" one looked very poor. Similarly, this is how your body reacts to words! You have to cherish positive words because they have more value. Treasuring the power of words was my first step forward in healing.

My wish was my command. I wanted to work around surgery and medication, and I did. I won my healing battle! It's not that I'm totally against medication. There is a time and place for medication, but it wouldn't suffice for my condition. My body reacted adversely to it. I empowered myself with positivity, realistic goals, and self-reliance. I knew I could do anything in the world once I healed. I found many healers to work with on my journey. They have helped me plant the seed of my healing tree. I have sprouted new budded branches to symbolize growth and recovery. My healers helped me blossom into a better person all across the board, making me feel more grounded than ever. They helped me sprout new wings and soar to new heights with recovery. Once you have solidified the foundation of your life, your whole body functions better and you can master the art of simplicity. With a solid foundation planted by my tree's roots, I kept my feet firmly planted while reaching for the stars. (Stay tuned for more about these extraordinary healers in upcoming chapters.)

Life is full of choices and the results of the choices we make. I want you, the reader, to understand how healing naturally is completely possible and how you can rise above any occasion. Just like I did, you need to trust in the process. Answers to your questions don't need to be found in a little brown bottle! I took gradual steps daily, and after years in the making, I am moving gracefully, walking taller, and dancing more freely toward my pain-free goal. I was, and still am, beaming with enthusiasm with all that I am learning in terms of natural health care. Now, I want you to be just as excited too!

CHAPTER 2:

My Changing Life and the Start of My Healing Journey

My new routine was a special version of a triathlon. I participated in grueling and relentless drills that included running from
home, to work, to doctor appointments all while in pain. I had always
dreamed of participating in a triathlon, but not in this way, shape, or
form! I was in motion like a madwoman on a mission—a pain-free
healing mission, that is.

My new recovery goal reminded me of my trip to the rainforest
of Puerto Rico in 2000. I was initiated into the natural healing world
on this trip. I practiced yoga, juice cleansed, and hiked through
the rainforest. I participated in complete body cleansing. My days
were packed with eating healthily, lots of exercise, and wholesome
activities. Each morning was started with a shot of wheatgrass juice
followed by meditation near a pretty stream. I ate a raw food diet
throughout the day and noshed on energy soups.

People on the retreat told me about Nancy, a colonic specialist
who I was encouraged to visit when I got back to New York. Colonics
help maintain your overall health. I set up an appointment with
Nancy for a colonic as soon as I was back home.

In my newly injured state, it was time to visit Nancy again. I
had seen Nancy for years before my accident, but now I had more
reasons to get colonics. The OxyContin I took had additional side
effects like constipation. Perfect timing for a colonic to give me
some relief!

If you've never had a colonic, I highly recommend them as part
of your preventive healthcare routine. I just wish that health insurance companies felt the same way about colonics. I've had over a

hundred colonics in my lifetime as part of my cleansing routine, and I feel great after each one.

Getting ready to leave the house for my first post-accident appointment with Nancy was scary! I barely recognized myself in the mirror and the pain was terrible. I eagerly arrived at Nancy's office, ready to go. As soon as I stepped into the candlelit office that morning, I was met with positive energy, the aroma of nice therapeutic oils, and ambient music for relaxation. I had a feeling that something exciting and healing-tastic was going to happen. Nancy greeted me with a welcoming smile. On that day, seeing Nancy was like meeting an angel. I told her about my bodybuilding accident and explained my persistent pain. I said I needed to wean myself off the medication and wanted to find doctors who would work with my fragile state. Nancy believed in my quest of pain-free living. We talked more about the specifics of my injuries and how I wanted to avoid surgery.

She asked, "Have you been to any natural healers?"

I said, "Not yet."

Nancy said, "I think I know someone who can help you."

Meeting with Nancy that day reminded me that other treatments were out there, ready for me to find.

I was open to Nancy's suggestion and thrilled to hear about this natural healing approach. She informed me how natural healers use holistic methods to help patients with their ailments. I had realized this in the past and had seen natural healers for physical maintenance. I had a feeling that this could help me. Natural healers favor alternative treatments over medication and invasive surgeries. These individualized practices include Reiki, herbal medicine, reflexology, homeopathy, acupuncture, Rolfing, and Traditional Chinese Medicine, just to name a few. This was what I was looking for!

Nancy earned her guardian angel standing and recommended chiropractor Dr. Kerr, whose office was close to my workplace. She predicted that he could lessen my pain without medication or surgery. I needed to get in touch with his office as soon as possible! I trusted Nancy's judgment because she was a wealth of information on the holistic side of healing.

At this point, I was in dire condition and would do anything to get rid of the pain. I was grateful for Nancy's suggestion. I was clueless about how Dr. Kerr's chiropractic practices would differ from the traditional care I was getting, but I knew that the pain wasn't going to go away by itself. I was so distressed and I had to find a solution.

I left Nancy and called Dr. Kerr's office. His chiropractic treatment sounded like a plan. I was eager and wanted in. After speaking to Nancy, I was inspired by her wise words about healers. I made an appointment with Dr. Kerr for the next day. I hung up the phone and prayed to God that this doctor would be the answer I sought.

Before starting this treatment, I still couldn't get out of bed without a pill. Each day was more strenuous than the last. Even the simplest task, such as walking from one room to the next, caused me incredible pain. And the pain was getting worse. My heart and intuition told me to start treatment with Dr. Kerr.

Astrologically speaking, I'm on the cusp of Leo and Virgo; I'm action-oriented and investigative. I like to involve those around me. I took a poll among my family and friends on whether I should see Dr. Kerr and take the holistic route. I was sure I would receive reassuring feedback, but I was surprisingly met with a resounding "no" all around.

My family warned me not to waste my money, to continue seeing a "real" doctor. The nearest and dearest to me thought that holistic doctors were not actual doctors. Even though they were all well aware about my suffering and pill dependence, they feared for my safety under the hands of alternative medicine. They knew how opposed I was to surgery, but they told me to stick with the pill program and continue with what I was already doing. I understood their apprehension, but they were not injured. I was the one hurting. I don't think they fully understood my dilemma. They were neither in pain nor addicted to pills. If I had to undergo surgery, I would be the only one on the operating table. My life was in danger, not theirs. They were all extremely unsupportive. However, I didn't actually care what they thought. I was just curious as to how shocked they'd be. I'm all about the shock value. I knew that natural healing was the most creative thing that I could do to restore my health. I was about to prove them all wrong. I confidently said to them, "Watch me heal myself holistically!"

I was ready for the next big step and anticipated my appointment with Dr. Kerr.

CHAPTER 3:

Dr. Kerr, the Hero

The first time I heard the word *chiropractic*, I pictured a cartoon man wincing in pain with lightning bolts shooting from his back, dying for relief! I soon learned that chiropractic treatments meant *way* more than that. Even though I felt like there were electrical shocks shooting into my body all the time, I soon learned there were more issues going on in my neck than previously diagnosed. I also learned that chiropractic treatment alleviates neck pain, manipulates the spine, enables pain management, and restores proper functionality to the nervous system.

My first trip to Dr. Kerr's Atlas of Life Chiropractic center was a milestone. I was *so* psyched for my appointment that I showed up 30 minutes early. I was at my wits' end, so desperate, and I could not live with pain any longer. Dr. Kerr was ready to see me and I hoped for the best. After a firm handshake and a confident smile, I felt comfortable in his presence. He was incredibly refined, focused, detailed, and well spoken. After he informed me that he could possibly help me, I had a feeling that he would become an integral character in my healing tale.

The first order of business on the docket was to take an X-ray of my skull. In the medical world where most doctors send patients to a lab for innumerable tests, Dr. Kerr performed all of the procedures himself. I appreciated his personalized approach. When I came to Dr. Kerr's office, I was in a lot of pain and had been struggling to decide whether to have surgery. He told me, "You may have to wind up getting surgery because your neck is badly hurt."

I asked, "Can this make it worse?"

He said it wouldn't exacerbate the situation, but it may not help. I trusted in the process anyway.

The X-ray revealed something the other doctors either missed or chose to overlook. He was the first doctor to identify the actual condition of why I was suffering. I was shocked with the results.

"Your skull is an inch off center," he told me.

I replied, "I don't understand. What does that mean?"

Dr. Kerr showed me the film that clearly pictured my slanted right eye, off center from where it should have been. Before he started explaining, it looked very bad. He said, "I found a terrible misalignment on your spine's first vertebrae that caused the rest of the spine to shift off."

I was floored.

That explained why one of my eyes was bulging outwards like a bullfrog. I asked Dr. Kerr if he could help me with this injury because I needed to get better, and he said we could try. I was so eager for him to help me and I was thrilled that he was able to diagnose my actual condition!

Here's a bit of background schema before we continue with the chapter. In Greek mythology, there is a giant by the name of Atlas. He and his fellow elders, the Titans, lost their war with the Greek gods. As punishment, Atlas was sentenced to bear the whole world on his shoulders for eternity. I once felt like I had the strength to lift the world. Now, on the flipside of things, my situation was comparable to the burdensome weight that Atlas felt.

Just like the mythical Atlas, there is a small bone located at the top of the spine right under your skull. In physiology, this bone is called the *C-1 vertebrae*. It is commonly referred to as the *Atlas bone*. This small, two-ounce bone supports the entire human head that can weigh between nine and seventeen pounds. Because the Atlas Bone carries all of this weight, it needs to be in a neutral or orthogonal position. This means that it should be at a 90-degree angle to the head and neck to keep the rest of the spine aligned.

So, what did this mean for my neck injury and me? I learned from Dr. Kerr that if the Atlas bone is misaligned by even a few degrees, the muscles holding up the head have to work harder, leading to overcompensation. With this issue, blockage occurs around the spinal cord. The nerves that affect all parts of the body do not work properly. Additional injuries in the neck, back, and other extremities can develop as well. I suffered from each and every one of the listed issues. I finally found what was causing my pain. Dr. Kerr's ability to find the cause of my problems made him a hero!

Dr. Kerr told me that anything from a car accident, to a fall, to a sports injury could cause your Atlas bone to shift from its orthogonal position. It's the most movable vertebra in the spine, pivoting around the second cervical vertebra called the axis. Unlike the rest of the spine, there is no disc between the Atlas and the vertebrae, just ligaments and tendons. This positioning allows spinal rotation, but at the price of instability. If you suffer from chronic pain in your back, neck, or shoulders, it could be years before you are diagnosed correctly. It is unlikely for a misaligned Atlas bone to show up in average medical tests. The only way I found out about the misalignment was when I went to Dr. Kerr because he specializes in these types of injuries.

While learning more about my injuries from Dr. Kerr, I found out that spinal crookedness could also be caused by physical, chemical, and/or emotional stress. If left unchecked, it could eventually lead to numerous conditions from the irritation and/or tension near the brain stem, causing health issues such as high blood pressure, asthma, allergies, and digestive discomfort. Because of all the sensory nerves in the spine, these spinal misalignments can manifest as neck pain, stiffness, tension headaches, migraines, and vertigo.

Important organ function could also be affected. I was suffering from several of these side effects, too.

Dr. Kerr explained that, over time, this injury leads to increased pressure in your discs, muscle spasms, abnormal spinal fluid flow, and blood flow to the head that can make you feel really terrible. Spinal misalignment can also cause an overall imbalance in the body, resulting in bodily overcompensation. The body goes into overdrive to cope. A spinal curvature develops, where tight muscles grow on one side of the spine. Another result is a postural imbalance, such as a tilted head, high shoulder, high hip, and uneven leg lengths. Over time, this poor positioning could lead to advanced forms of bone degeneration, back and shoulder pain, fusion of the vertebrae, and herniated discs. For me, the herniated discs were leaning on my spinal cord, giving me paralyzing pain on the right side of my body.

I had nowhere else to turn, and I was dying for relief. I was so grateful that Dr. Kerr agreed to help me. All of the things that he discussed with me fit my condition, diagnosis, and anguish precisely. Dr. Kerr rushed to my rescue (like any good superhero would) and got to the crux of my injuries. All he was missing was the special ensemble, complete with a cape and spandex!

During my first appointment, I laid down on the table and Dr. Kerr placed a metal pointed object, called the Atlas Orthogonal Percussion Adjusting Instrument, next to my ear. This device looked like a futuristic tool. I felt like this couldn't be happening in real life. It was like I was in a movie. Dr. Kerr pushed a button and the machine released gentle sound waves to move the skull back into place. The feeling of my skull moving was terrible, but I knew it would make me better! For a month, it was really difficult for me to even lie down on the instrument to get adjusted. I'd cry on the table because of the pain! After a few weeks, I started to feel like it was helping. It was exhilarating to find something that helped.

Dr. Kerr said to me, "If you want to keep going with this, let's see if we can avoid surgery."

Dr. Kerr did this same procedure several times during my visits, resting for ten-minute intervals before starting up again to move the skull into its normally centered position. When he was done, I was relieved, for I felt it was a work in progress. The pain shooting down my arm lessened in intensity and occurred less frequently. Dr. Kerr was pleased with how I was healing. It took about a month for me to get out of that initial pain. If we were talking on a pain scale of 1-10, my level was way over a 10. I had severe neck pain, both arms were numb, my right one hurting worse than the left one, and I couldn't feel my hands. Everything hurt, and with Dr. Kerr, I was finding some sort of relief. Tears of joy streamed down my face, as I finally found an alternative form of pain management.

This relief came at a hefty cost. While I was fortunate enough to discover a treatment that actually worked, this wasn't covered under my medical insurance. This meant that I would have to pay out of my own pocket to see Dr. Kerr. I had bills to pay and children who were financially dependent on me. I needed to think positively and stick to my gut feeling about continuing this treatment. He was the only doctor in New York City who did this type of work and I needed it badly. My bank account was getting drained, but it was worth the investment to say the least.

I continued my new healing plan with Dr. Kerr, which was just what I was looking for. Meeting Dr. Kerr was a turning point in my life. I was so honored to be in his presence. I told him that if he could help with pain management and healing, I'd write a book to chronicle my journey to tell my story to the universe and help others. I began regaining my health with this treatment. It made me realize how injured I really was. I started thinking about other people who are victimized by pain on a daily basis and wanted to share my experiences with the world. And alas, *Happy Healing* was born! I'd go to his office every morning at 8:00 a.m. to receive treatment because I was so eager to find relief. Sometimes I'd even call him on Saturdays and Sundays for an appointment and he would come through and help me on weekends, always caring for me. He changed my life forever and is my hero today, a protagonist in my life story. I really took charge of my health. I made the decision to not have neck surgery, even when doctors told me I would not be able to find another way, I succeeded!

At this point, the subway ride back to Brooklyn started to bother me, making me sore from all the jostling. I decided to move to Manhattan to be closer to work and treatment. In the weeks following my first session with Dr. Kerr, I packed up my belongings, left my beloved Brooklyn house, and fled to Manhattan. My children were in their 20s and always busy. They were old enough to look after themselves. My intuitive self made this move because I knew it was in my best interest, simplifying things.

Moving from Brooklyn to Manhattan was quite the transition. I began settling into my new 600-sq. ft. studio apartment. Instead of having expansive windows that overlooked a tree-lined street, I had a small terrace with enough room for four chairs and a table. I had a nice view of the street and the MetLife building. The locale was ideal! Downstairs were restaurants, galleries, and small hotels filled with tourists, a far cry from my quiet neighborhood in Brooklyn. I felt ritzy and chic.

I liked that I didn't have to take public transportation. I loved how all my destinations were within walking distance. Not getting shaken by the train meant less pain, and at the same time, less time with family. However, getting rid of pain was my primary objective. I was intent on avoiding surgery and it made sense to relocate where my commute to the office was within walking distance.

Time flew by even quicker in Manhattan and six months had already passed where I only traveled on foot. Walking provided some relief. It became my go-to exercise because I could no longer do any physical training in the gym or work out on the elliptical. The day regretfully came where I surrendered and finally had my children sell my treasured Precor machine on eBay. I shed some tears when I received a phone call that the machine's new owner had come to pick it up. Letting the machine go was like giving away a treasured part of myself. It was the end of my bodybuilding era.

Six months into this treatment, my neck went out of whack again, right back to the old, terrible feeling. I was freaked out because all of a sudden, I was in major pain again. I remember crying on the phone to my father because I was in agony. My father told me to listen to the doctors and get the surgery. A friend of his had four herniated discs, went through with the surgery, and was recovering nicely.

I asked him, "Was the friend wearing a neck brace?"

And he said, "Yes—you should go through with the surgery."

I refused. I did not want to be cut open with the inherent risks involved.

I wondered if I needed to bite the bullet and stop my holistic treatments. In the emergency room, they would give me morphine and prepare for immediate surgery. I knew that my only other choice was to continue Dr. Kerr's treatment. I believed in Dr. Kerr's solution because I had always been an advocate of natural healing and my instincts felt that this was still the best option. I went back to Dr. Kerr and demanded him to adjust me again. Even though Dr. Kerr advised that his treatment could not really help because of my severe condition, I was once again in an urgent situation. He told me to go straight to the hospital, but I said, "No way!" I insisted he help me and continue with the treatment. So, he alleviated the pain once more.

With Dr. Kerr's help, I started recovering. Eventually, I was able to have the prescription for OxyContin downgraded back to Percocet. That, in and of itself, was progress.

CHAPTER 4:

Adding Some Structural Integration

I continued to see my hero Dr. Kerr. He was my hero for diagnosing my problem, providing a tactical treatment plan for a potential pain-free solution. Like my pill addiction, I was similarly becoming addicted to his treatment. Between living in my new apartment, walking everywhere, and feeling better, I was almost pain-free! Even though my bank account balance was dipping lower and lower from each treatment, I embraced this new normalcy because my life was really starting to look brighter. Everything was going so well that I practically forgot what pain felt like.

Suddenly, on November 2, 2010, eruptions of pain shot through my lower back. The pain was now worse than ever. I was in regression, all the way back to where I started.

Yikes! Before I knew it, I was taking Percocet again four times per day. I could not function without them. My routine looked like this: I'd wake up and reach for the pills. I practically inhaled them and waited 20 minutes for the wave of relief to hit. With the pills always within an arm's reach, I crawled to work and sessions with Dr. Kerr.

My main priority of the day was to numb the pain, so I continued popping pills. Those little prescribed brown bottles were my only source of comfort to hold me over between Dr. Kerr's treatment sessions. I didn't know what else to do. My holistic treatments were not helping 100% of the time. I was still working and maintaining my great level of stick-to-itiveness. Those pills gave me a false sense of security, which I did not enjoy. A couple of weeks back into my vicious Percocet cycle, my friend accused me of being "a victim of the pill." He was right. I needed additional options to work with to avoid being addicted to medication for life.

During my next session with Dr. Kerr, I expressed my recent back pain. He explained that the pain in my neck was traveling down to my back, and he couldn't really help. I extensively researched other professionals who could offer natural cures to my new pain. I began seeing many alternative healers, and each of them gave me temporary relief. I was doing everything in my power to break my bond with prescription drugs. I knew I had the strength to do so. I once again had to garner the strength and perseverance of my astrological sign, Leo/Virgo. It's not in my DNA to give up easily. Every new healer and technique I found kept me going strong, finding ways to naturally end my misery.

My next strategy was Rolfing. I visited Kate Hildebrandt, a Rolfing Structural Integration expert. This treatment manipulates soft tissue and uses movement to realign the body. This technique was invented over 50 years ago and is still as current as ever. I hoped this would cure my back.

Kate was the Director of Operations for a large law firm in the 1980s. She was led to Rolfing after years of dissatisfaction with her corporate job. Kate had Rolfing practitioner friends who loved what they did, and she was inspired to pursue the practice.

Kate told me, "I was frustrated with how the medical world treated my whiplash. I suffered for so many years. I thought massages and chiropractic treatment would work, but these did not resolve my issue. When I found Structural Integration, I started off with 10 sessions and paid out of pocket. I was cured! I came back from the sessions better than ever. I even have a great before-and-after picture of myself that I show to clients, and they can't believe that I was so rounded over. My back and my neck hurt so much! I was a mess."

Before whiplash, Kate was a scuba diver, backpacker, and cross-country skier. She went from doing everything to doing nothing. Kate related to my pain.

Many of Kate's clients have had deep tissue massage but did not reap long-lasting results. They have been temporarily healed. Their problem returns and starts hurting again, so they turn to Rolfing. When patients come to Kate, she says, "They've had chiropractic treatment, but it doesn't hold. I shape it and help it hold because soft tissue is like mud. With injuries, it becomes like stiff mud. The bones are like sticks and have no ability to fight the pattern that the soft tissue is putting on them. The spinal column and joints get jammed up. By working with the connective tissue, I allow the whole body to rehydrate itself. I use the bones as trail markers, to complete the sculpting process. People may come in with one single targeted area. I don't just focus on that one specific area. Rather, I focus on allowing the whole body to unwind by giving it specific information through Rolfing."

Kate explained that all structures' strengths lie in their foundations. If the foundation is not reinforced, then the entire thing will fail. For example, if a tree's trunk is damaged, then the tree is unable to grow healthily, develop branches, and sprout leaves. She explained how her treatment would help my condition: her technique views the body as an ecosystem, where she manipulates the deep soft tissues to alleviate ailments. Rolfing helps restore and realign the underlying network of connective tissues through massage. This treats muscle pain and tension, where each session focuses on a specific body part. Her treatments were incredible! They felt like a deep tissue massage. She helped rub out the tightness, manage the chronic pain, and made my bones feel better! It was a relief!

How does Rolfing target the way the body operates? The connection of the tissue is like a 3-D spider web that starts at the soles of your feet and surrounds each muscle. The hamstring has three pieces. The connective tissue surrounds each piece, goes through each part of the spider web, and acts as a pin and ligament at the end. It bundles and enables us to be connected. The connective tissue goes all the way up to your head.

Upon my first visit in 2011, I complained about my back problems. Kate helped take pressure off my back. Kate worked around my spine to help hydrate the connective tissue, bone structure, and soft tissue and made space for them. Rolfing gave my body a nice support system because the back essentially supports the whole body! She manipulated my body to move my back's tissue and loosen the fascia that was tight from muscle strain. The tissues, including blood, ligaments, and tendons, in our body are all interconnected. Fascia is the tissue that envelops our entire structures as well as intersperses itself within the muscle fibers. This tissue has a collagenous, sheath-like consistency. Fascia also joins at each muscle's endpoints where ligaments and tendons develop and attach the muscle to the bone. At this point, fascia was an important term for me to learn during my healing journey. Loosening my body's fascia became one of my goals because it enables physical freedom.

Because the layers of fascia encase our muscles and merge through the entire body, our system is multi-layered. Thus, any bodily strain creates a reaction with the rest of the body. For example, stress felt in the leg's connective tissue can pull that tissue around your torso and other body parts. With my condition, I needed to eliminate this internal bodily stress that I felt in my back and to create more internal space for all of my systems, including the fascial system, enabling expansiveness.

When the body is at a normal and balanced state, the fascial tissue is moveable, moist, and fluid. This enables movement in the body. Conversely, under different circumstances, such as less motion and pressure, the fascia becomes stiff and immobile. The fascia starts to attach itself to other tissues in the body and can be felt as adhesions. I was suffering from stiff fascia. Before I met Kate, I did not know that the condition of my rigid fascial system stunted my own recovery inside and out.

During one of my sessions, Kate discovered that I was walking with an outwardly extended right leg. My right foot was turned outward and looked like a stiff hockey stick. She told me that this resulted from the imbalances in my lower back. Kate explained, "Rolfing is like architecture for the body. If the feet and legs are the foundation of the body and they aren't grounding you properly, then you are unbalanced." Your upper body that is made up of the head, ribcage, pelvis, and spine has a lot of volume. It is very heavy. If the bottom of the body does not correctly support your upper half, things could go wrong. It's like building a house without putting the basement in.

My right leg was turning out because my body was stuck in that pattern. During the session, Kate said that she sees these patterns all the time with different clients. Either people's feet are turned out on both sides, or turned in, or one side is turned out. Kate helped me correct my right foot to a more supportive stance. And you can't just say you can change it easily because my right foot was stuck in a pattern. My body was comfortable in that pattern—stuck as part of a long-term problem.

"Sometimes these issues are because of an accident, or even a genetic pattern." Kate said, "You see little kids that have the same body patterns as their parents. This sort of thing, like the outward-turned foot, happens a lot."

Kate explained, "By focusing on that right foot and allowing it to be a column of support to ground the leg, the whole body began to feel better. If one side is twisted, it twists everything up the line. This situation helped a much bigger picture."

Rolfing's simplicity implemented focused healing instructions for my body to follow. I realigned my body while releasing emotional issues. After seeing Kate for six months, I noticed dramatic progress with my stance. Instead of hunching, I started walking with a straighter right leg. Kate was a doll to work with. I loved going to her treatments, and they felt wonderful. I felt so alive when I came out of Rolfing because it got the blood flowing. She helped me fight the patterns that my soft tissue was stuck in. I was in a better space after Rolfing. But, I was still taking medicine and not yet fully healed.

CHAPTER 5:

Body Tuning with Terrific Dr. Tatz

My next stop was to Dr. Shmuel Tatz, another recommendation from my friend Nancy. This internationally renowned doctor is a physical therapist who specializes in Body Tuning. Body Tuning is like bodywork, but functions on a more advanced level. Dr. Tatz has treated an internationally diverse group of people. His extensive clientele includes an array of artists, musicians, actors, dancers, yogis, and former bodybuilders (people just like me). I entered his office and was impressed by the assortment of signed celebrity memorabilia that sung his praises, thanking him for a job well done. I knew that if he could help these people, he'd be able to help me too.

Dr. Tatz studied physical therapy and medical exercise in college. In the 1970s, he worked with the Soviet Olympic team to hone his injury treatment abilities, and he took additional bodywork classes to integrate massage in his own practice. Since his beginnings, he's developed an interesting practice.

After my first visit, complete with an evaluation, I wanted to sign up for sessions. He informed me that I had to see him twice a week for a total of 12 sessions. I practically emptied my bank account again with hopes of a pain-free life. He told me that this treatment could help the body avoid surgery entirely.

With over 40 years of experience, Dr. Tatz is basically a wizard. He has the training to know exactly what's going on and views the body as an instrument by observing the patient and assessing where the body needs work. Dr. Tatz intently listens to the body with his hands and makes fine tunings where necessary to regulate the body's wellbeing. He uses reflex-physiotherapy and uses acupuncture points to feel all the body's ailments and manipulate them for maximum patient recovery. From lower back and neck pain to sinusitis and insomnia, the talented Dr. Tatz treats it all. He's a master of his trade, and as Dr. Tatz puts it, "My tools are my hands." Taking elements of Western physical therapy treatments and Eastern healing arts, he helps people ease their pain and he gives them peace of mind.

Dr. Tatz has a distinct philosophy when approaching patients. He explains, "Each person has different complaints. I want to talk directly with the problem to see what is going on. I look at the patient's body and observe its movements. I try different techniques and do a series of manipulations: I move the skin, tissue, muscles, bones, and ligaments, to see how the mechanics of your body work. I listen to what the body is telling me what to do. I listen to the joint sounds and the muscle sounds. My hands feel and my ears listen and tell me what is wrong. Then I explain to the patient what is going on with their body and help them."

In discussion with Dr. Tatz, he compared the body to a machine, like a car: "When it works, it works. When it doesn't work, it needs to be tuned up. Just like a machine. The interesting thing that makes us different from machines is that we have a brain, and in order to be tuned, we need to use our brain. Healing is a full body experience. Through enough diligence, hard work, and time, the person can recover." He means that we, as human beings, can rev up our engines with care to function at full capacity. And of course with a full tank of fuel, I might add!

In addition to physical therapy, he also specializes in auricular therapy, an Asian practice that increases circulation in the body. Similar to acupuncture, the ears are massaged to stimulate specific body parts, organs, glands, and tissues. Because the ears contain a complex set of reflex nerve connections, the flow of healing energy increases around the body. These reflexes stimulate the production of neurotransmitters, like endorphins, that enable the body to feel better.

He performed diapulse, a technique where electromagnetic fields target injured body parts to stimulate regeneration and to protect the neurons. It vibrates the body to promote functionality of the circulatory system. When injured, it is common for your system to suffer from poor circulation. I too had this issue. I found this method to be extremely effective.

The first time Dr. Tatz wheeled out the machine, I thought I was in a sci-fi movie because the apparatus looked über advanced. Was I about to get shock treatment? Or was I perhaps getting beamed into space? The device was so bizarre and intimidating! When Dr. Tatz explained that diapulse actually restores the red and white blood cells, stimulates blood flow, and reduces swelling in tissue, I was looking forward to seeing how I would feel after the treatment. I soon learned how the whole bodily process of increased blood flow works when catalyzed by the stimulation of veins, capillaries, nerves, and the small arteries. Dr. Tatz's special skills were what I needed to get all of these parts flowing.

By the time my third visit rolled around, the pain was finally gone! Because I had no pain, I was walking on cloud nine! After three months of these sessions, I was able to function without painkillers! For me, this was a dramatic improvement. No wonder why all the famous folk sang his praises!

When helping patients heal, Dr. Tatz suggests additional treatments based on what the client's body is telling him. He said, "Healing is individualized. I can tell what each person needs depending on his or her specific problem and what their body feels like. The body tells me how it needs to heal." He recommended a treatment I never thought of before. Something so natural and rudimentary: jazz dance classes! Apparently, my body spoke to him and said I needed to get a move on and loosen up. Dancing would also help me avoid additional pain and be a form of physical therapy.

Dr. Tatz's treatment worked wonders and cured my back. I kept going back to him. I was persistent with this treatment because medicine was not an option.

He knew I would listen to his advice, how movement is crucial to healing. We need to maintain our bodies' optimal health on a daily basis. As we get older, bodily upkeep becomes more and more important. It is this simple: Without motion, you are stagnant and there is no room for growth and development. If you stay in motion, you'll be okay. I saw this firsthand with my parents and how they stayed in great shape by placing emphasis on staying healthy over the years. My father inspired me to be mobile because he stayed extremely active all throughout his life, even during his mid-90s! I admire his willpower greatly! He went on the elliptical every day for 45 minutes. I would soon put my mobile limits to the test and learn that with movement, if you don't use it, you lose it. Sounds cliché, but true.

The thought of myself dancing seemed ludicrous. I didn't seem like the jazzy-snazzy-dance type of person. Besides, I couldn't even touch my toes or tap my toes to the beat of a song. But dancing was worth the try. I was ready to try *anything*.

CHAPTER 6:

Dancing with Henri, the Star

Sure, I've always loved music, any type of music, and secretly yearned to have moves like Jagger, but I never planned to actualize my dream to become a dancer. Following Dr. Tatz's jazz dance suggestion, I came across a dance instructor named Henri Velandia. He looked like la crème de la crème in the world of dance—a very spiritual, in-tune, and interesting gentleman. From my first lesson, I knew I had found the right teacher to help with my next steps of recovery. When you dance, you become more in touch with yourself. Your body follows suit and heals with an open mind. It's an all-encompassing experience of the body, mind, and soul.

I soon learned that dancing is one of the most liberating things you can do in your life, making you fly and choose and explore the world differently. In my case of recovery, dance gave me wings to naturally heal. Like a bird, I was able to soar to new heights above the ground, above the trees, and I could revel in this newfound freedom that provided me with a bird's eye view of my situation and injuries. This new perspective helped me communicate more directly with my body, pinpoint the pain, and dance it out of my system.

And, hey, the entire world is a stage. You might as well do a mean dance routine on that stage, improvise a bit from the knowledge you've gained, and own every minute of it, especially when in stages of recovery.

When I first met Henri, I knew he was a star. At that time, he became the guiding star in my sky and a superstar in my life. His shining presence gave me confidence about this suitable recovery method. Because Henri emitted positivity, we clicked immediately.

So, I started with jazz, an umbrella term that includes many styles like Latin jazz. Before I started dance classes, I couldn't even touch my toes or wiggle them.

During my first lesson with Henri, I told him about my injuries and hope to recover through natural healing and dance. Henri told me, "We can use movement in jazz to get the body's mobility up-and-running." I saw Henri's moves and wanted to move like him, so I scheduled private lessons! That was the start of our great journey.

I arrived at Henri's apartment in Harlem at 7:00 a.m. for four hours a week, leaving my apartment at the crack of dawn to accommodate both our schedules. From my injuries, I was very stiff. Take a second from reading and imagine Frankenstein in a dance class. Yep, for my first year of dancing, that's exactly what I looked like. I still feel like Frankenstein sometimes but that doesn't stop me. It is not an overnight process. My steps were harsh, I had limited mobility, and I looked half-dead because of the stagnant energy in my body. But I still loved working with Henri.

In the beginning, it was quite the struggle. I fought the changes that my body was trying to undergo through dance. I kept having the urge to take pills to numb the pain from breaking in my muscles activated by dance. The average person would just stop the process and settle for pills. I couldn't accept that option. When you take the medication, your body is constricted. It doesn't breathe properly and you don't heal. I controlled my pill-popping impulses and kept on shuffling with my boogie shoes.

Slowly but surely, I started to feel better. I was maintaining my body's free flow without having any pain in my back. It was excellent, so I continued my study of dance. Through these different forms of dance, Henri helped me gain flexibility and enabled me to work on my body's fluidity, on my path of physical freedom.

One of Henri's favorite styles of dance is Zen Zouk. This sensual, full-body Brazilian dance promotes alignment. By guiding your natural energies through dance, you can achieve freedom through movement and expression. With practice, you can become strong and flexible, open up your mind, and learn how to communicate with your body. It also teaches the art of breathing to relax your body. With these tools I learned from dance class, I trained myself to avoid medication and breathe through the pain. I was soon dancing through life. I became more lighthearted and relaxed; essentially, I was pain-free. And even more importantly, I was having the time of my life! Dancing was my newfound passion. I found it to be a cathartic experience, and it helped me get to the core of my problems.

Dancing helped me reset the beat of my life's newfound rhythm, complete with a strong bass line, lead guitars, and a powerhouse vocal range, all performed by me, of course! All of these things were possible through breathing and movement. Who would have thought that healing would start to be fun once the pain subsided?! Henri helped me reach for the stars, set new goals in my recovery path, and breathe new life into my healing path.

Dance has always been a huge part of superstar Henri's life. He is always evolving through his choreography, performances, and teaching. He specializes in many different styles of dance. His list includes salsa, Latin jazz, bachata, modern dance, contemporary, ballroom, and Brazilian Zen Zouk.

Henri's jazz class infuses Latin rhythms with movement. He said, "My instructing techniques work on the body, mind, and spirit. I help students form physical and mental confidence. With my students, I emphasize free body expression through movement."

Henri said I'm the most determined student he's ever had. When we worked together, I inspired him because I was such a go-getter. Each class, we explored new movements and made strides on my road to recovery. Henri recognized how I always found new revelations about my wellbeing. He stated, "Deb, you're so motivated to learn and you never give up." I've made mind-blowing progress!

Henri gave encouraging advice during class. I like to do everything fast because I'm so enthusiastic to learn. Henri encouraged me to take my time, slow it down, and do all the motions. When learning to slow down the movements, I can more closely connect with every part of my body to promote recovery. Through this, I began developing a broader range of motion and have been building momentum with my progress.

Henri taught me that dance should be very organic and should engage the entire body. Through Henri's dance experiences, he has always felt the energy flowing in his body. The first time I thought about it, I felt the energy manifesting in my spine too. These energy points are so important when dancing.

Henri said, "When you're dancing, you are tapping into different emotions associated with different parts of your body. For example, when dancing about the emotion of 'love,' you're connecting with your chest/heart. Also, different parts of the body engage with an emotion, a color, and a chakra. I found that these energy points are so important when studying dance. When you are tapping into these different emotions, dancing becomes even more spiritual."

Henri's philosophy describes how the body is your own place of energy flow. He explains, "With the dance I teach, I encourage my students to be aware of seven elements. Mastery of breathing, energy flow, and these elements helps my students get to the next level." Bringing the mind, body, and spirit together through dance and these elements has really helped my recovery. Here are the seven elements in great detail:

Earth: Take total control of your ground, your roots.

Water: Master the "sensuality" within your essence.

Fire: Nothing can stop you from your will and determination.

Air: Fly beyond expectations, releasing the power of your wings.

Vibration: Express your true self.

Animal: Connect to the intuition of your soon-to-be-awakened animal.

Kingdom: Become the ruler of your temple. "Your body."

At this point in my healing story, I was 100% medication-free. What astounding progress I made!

CHAPTER 7:

Breathing Through the Rising Pressure

After being totally free from the awful pain medication, I finally thought I had tamed the beast, aka my health. In January 2011, I happily went to my primary doctor for a standard checkup. I anticipated to pass my checkup with flying colors and I looked forward to flaunting my healing progress, showing how healthy I was becoming.

The nurse took my height, weight, and temperature; the nurse even remarked how I looked younger! Dancing was working wonders for me! Next on the agenda was the blood pressure test. Much to my dismay, I was told I had high blood pressure; my vitals read 160 over 90. I didn't feel any differently. Because I was taking great care and honoring my body, how could I have developed high blood pressure?

This made me so nervous. I was practically shaking in my seat. I couldn't believe the reading, so I asked the nurse to take my blood pressure again. She took it three more times, and got the same numbers. I still couldn't fathom it. The nurse suggested I go outside, take a stroll, and come back in five minutes. I took this time to read my emails and received an email from a client who finally mailed a check that was three weeks late. This news was a relief! I went back into the office, and when the nurse rechecked my pressure, it went back to normal—for the time being.

That wasn't the end of my blood pressure problems. A year later, I had another wake-up call about my health when my aunt fell ill. In the summer of 2013, my aunt fainted in the middle of the night while she was returning from a trip to the bathroom. I was there when she was rushed to the hospital, and she ended up being admitted for high blood pressure. She had already been taking two high blood pressure pills, two cholesterol medications, a sleeping pill, and a pill to control her bladder in the evenings. That day, she accidently mixed up all her medicines because she did not take them at the right times. It was terrible! When you get to a certain age, your body shuts down and becomes stagnant. I refused to get to that point and just live with high blood pressure. I would take healing into my own hands.

While there in the hospital with my aunt, I asked the nurse to take my blood pressure because I wasn't feeling well. I had the chills and felt very lightheaded. My blood pressure was 190 over 90. I told my aunt, "Move over! I'm getting in bed with you!" When I was in the hospital, I felt horrible! My aunt took pills and felt better after an hour. This situation freaked me out. I feared for my aunt's health and my own. Lying there with my medicated aunt, it hit me. This was a wake-up call to care for my body even more, take further precautions, and keep up my holistic approach.

I went to see my primary physician who wanted me to take medication to monitor my situation for immediate relief. I said, "Are you kidding me? I'm never taking meds again!" If I chose to take this medication (which I didn't), I would be in the same situation as my elderly aunt. Like my aunt, I would be addicted for life. I needed to find alternative answers to my high blood pressure just like I did with my neck and back pain. My family wanted me to listen to the doctors, like my aunt did, and take the medication, but I needed to do what my heart was telling me to do for a healthy life. No prescriptions for me this time around! I was proud to steer clear of the situation. I solved this problem with one of the easiest things—the power of breath.

Up until this point, I was breathing, but not truly *breathing*. Who knew that breathing was something you had to "learn" to do?! I was instinctively bringing air through my body in a mindless manner. Because of my bodybuilding prowess, air in my muscles was practically nonexistent. I now know that this was due to the inadequate blood flow occurring in my body. My brain was not getting enough oxygen to send healing signals to the rest of my body. When my bodybuilding accident happened, my hands and toes were scary-looking, lifeless, like those of a corpse. The circulation in my body was extremely poor, causing high blood pressure.

Breathing is such an important facet of life that people take for granted. I know I might sound like the master of the obvious by this statement, but please take it seriously. Specifically, when taking restorative measures with your body, the most important thing is not forgetting to breathe! I turned to Henri's classes to dance through the issue. When I updated Henri about my newly developed high blood pressure problems, he told me to breathe, just as we had practiced.

A few days later after dance class, I ordered a glass of wine at my favorite Italian restaurant, Zero Otto Nove on 21st St. between 5th and 6th Avenues in New York City. The bartender, Fred, opened a new wine bottle and poured me a glass. It didn't taste right.

Fred said, "Debbie, it's got to breathe. It's a new bottle."

I laughed and said, "We all have to breathe." But the bottles, just like humans, really need time to breathe correctly.

With proper maintenance, people can age like fine wine. People, like wine, have to breathe to reach their full potential. Especially when focusing on pushing air into my injured places and allowing for healing to take place, I looked at breathing differently. Respiration was no longer a proper life function occurring unconsciously. Rather, it became a more mindful exercise that I worked on, and dancing definitely helped me understand this concept.

Through the ages, breathing practices have been explored in different cultures. There are ancient practices that acknowledge the power and wisdom of breath. Ancient yogis in India associated breathing with healing, an important practice when seeking results in your life's path. The Taoist philosophy believes that learning how to breathe like a child in the womb can help you unlock your subconscious later on in life and overcome obstacles that presently hold you back.

In ancient Asia, people believed that air was the basis for all living beings and crucial for healing. The Sanskrit term "prana" means "life source" and refers to the vital energy required by the body to function on a heightened level. Pranayama, or the exercise of breath control, creates energy currents to control functions happening in the body. Pranayama is a fundamental aspect of yoga (which you'll hear about my yogi practices in a later chapter), as well as other mind/body healing techniques. When we become mindful of our breathing, it becomes even more powerful. Prana promotes recovery from injuries, healthy digestion, blood circulation, and mood. It works in tandem with the body, mind, and spirit to heal physical and emotional trauma. The restorative effect that it has on the body essentially cleanses the system, provides pain relief, and enables freedom.

We need to focus on our breathing to circulate the oxygen around to each part of our body to really feel a stretch, heal the body, or lower blood pressure. I didn't fully understand how necessary this concept was until I started my work with Henri. While dancing Henri's signature style, Zen Zouk, I was introduced to the proper way to breathe: to close my eyes, breathe in deeply through my nose, and focus on letting the air fill my head and stomach. Then, I exhale from my belly button and release tension. Breath control, when combined with proper body alignment, makes your natural energy forces achieve freedom. All of these elements allow your body to express itself and relax. This type of breathing helped me to manage my back pain as well. Henri's breath and dance techniques placed me in a better stage of healing. By practicing conscious breathing as I danced, I filled my body with the air I needed to naturally feel better.

Just after my high blood pressure incident with my aunt, I had another injury. I popped the Achilles tendon in my heel during a stretching session. I hurt it because I pushed too hard to get the oxygen flowing. I took it easy and it healed within a few weeks and I was taking a much gentler approach.

I learned how to monitor blood pressure and breathing on my own. My pressure first read 180 over 90. After completing this breathing technique over time, I began retaking my pressure. The apparatus read 125 over 80. Bringing my blood pressure down like this proved that if I controlled my breathing, I had it made!

Before I learned to breathe properly, my hands and feet were discolored from poor blood circulation. I could not wiggle my toes because they were so stiff. Because of the breathing changes, my feet looked better too! After this journey, I'm still working on separating my toes that always had limited mobility. I feel incredible by simply controlling my breath flow. Moments like these have become milestones in my path of physical freedom!

In Henri's own words, here's how he defines breathing: "Breath is the essence of life. Without breath, you are not alive. Like in life, breathing is also a key component of dance. When you're challenged in life, the body's natural instinct is to hold its breath. It's like a form of defense. Not many people know you can overcome this instinct through dance and breathing. This is because breath and movement work together. You have to learn to breathe through challenges, in life and on the dance floor. All of these elements make you a stronger person." One must breathe through their difficulties, rather than tense up, and focus on working them out.

Henri taught me the power of growth through breath. "When you hold your breath, it stunts your growth. In order to develop, you need to breathe because it helps the body relax. It is a full body experience. When you are breathing, your body can expand and contract and you can feel the blood flowing throughout your veins. With breath control, you can breathe air and life into your muscles and allow them to soothe. Through breathing, muscle memory develops.

With enough airflow in the body, the muscles, mind, and body grow together and heal."

Henri suggested I should take a deeper look into my troubles. He had a solution to keep me moving forward and he knew of a talented person who could help me.

CHAPTER 8:

Achieving the Art of Alignment

While still rocking and rolling at dance classes with Henri, he suggested I see Anne-Marie Duchêne, founder and owner of Art of Alignment. Henri raved about her, saying how I would be changed by her work. Anne-Marie had helped Henri recover from overexertion. He has extremely high standards, so if Anne-Marie's program received his stamp of approval, I knew I had to work with her. I was so excited to meet Anne-Marie!

Through her specialization in Hellerwork Structural Integration, people like me can get relief from chronic joint and muscle pain. This type of therapy involves therapeutic dialogue, movement rehabilitation, and connective tissue manipulation techniques to realign and unify the mind/body experience. It's amazing how Anne-Marie puts her own personal flair in her practice, making it even more tailored to a person's specific needs!

Anne-Marie was fortunate enough to learn Hellerwork Structural Integration directly from the genius himself, Joseph Heller! Anne-Marie expanded Dr. Heller's work and added her own education in visceral manipulation, craniosacral skills, and osteopathic knowledge to create her practice. Anne-Marie said, "Adding these components in my practice has greatly enhanced my success rate with my treatments. I am also very much interested in the somatic psychology (body-oriented therapy) part of the work as well as shamanism (practices that can cure pain, forming relationships with the spirit realm). All of these elements assist me in my work to offer better and more complete healing modalities for my clients."

Anne-Marie is interested in integrating the allopathic medical system and the holistic system of healing because they are synergistically combined; they don't work separately. And isn't that how things work in life? As soon as we pull things apart, we ultimately want to return to a place of integration. It's how nature works all around us. For the most part, people want to reconcile with themselves and one another. Being at odds with someone inevitably creates chaos within us. Learning to take full responsibility and forgiveness is possible. Anne-Marie believes that this is instrumental for maintaining your health and functioning as a human being. Anne-Marie's work is "about awakening human potentiality and taking massive decisive action to get there. Gently, in loving-kindness, and with certainty."

During my first session with Anne-Marie, she told me that her purpose is to guide people in the direction of growing into their fully-fledged selves. First, we discussed my medical history, assessed my body's structure, posture, alignment, balance, and movement patterns. I booked 12 sessions! Anne-Marie talked to me about how I can improve my life and she performed special bodywork to help align my body. Working with her helped my pain management. On all ends of the spectrum, it was incredible. Instead of silencing the pain with numbing medication, we targeted my problem areas to let my injuries "speak." This tactic was so intriguing; we let them scream in anguish, we listened intently to their cries, and then we treated them accordingly. Score! Medication-free body = ecstatic Debra.

Hellerwork presumes that everyone is fundamentally healthy, but with our constantly changing lives, this stasis sometimes gets out of alignment. With enough attention to the body, realignment of the fascia will make a person feel better. Yes, I was practically worn out and started to feel better. That's where Anne-Marie helped me to relieve the discomfort and strengthen my long-term recovery.

Anne-Marie's practice specifically targeted my tension, stress, ergonomics, flexibility, posture, and breathing. To heal, the psychological, emotional, spiritual, and physical aspects must blend together to develop. Hellerwork uses an approach similar to Rolfing treatment to address fascia (the connective tissue) to proliferate good health, promote heightened energy levels, positive self-awareness, and a more stable body. Depending on our habits and level of movement, fascia can stick differently. The average person would guess that the tension, stiffness, and limited mobility they suffer from are correlated to the muscles. But in actuality, it is the connective tissue that amasses this strain. Because fascia is malleable, it can return to its original form with a treatment like Hellerwork.

In Anne-Marie's Hellerwork practice, she manipulates the physical body in her practice to create more space, from the inside out. Anne-Marie states, "A big focus of HSI is to work with the connective tissue of the human body. It differs from physical therapy, chiropractic, or any type of manual therapy that focuses on 'fixing' the body." Anne-Marie explains that this is "a gentle method of addressing the tissues within the body and allowing it to breathe more easily." This technique "supports the organic healing of the body and recognizes that the body is the inherent healer." Anne-Marie said, "Hellerwork uses therapeutic dialogue alongside the bodywork where we address the psyche, the emotions, and frequently the spiritual part of the person. The complete program realigns the human system, body, psyche, and emotions. Every session builds upon the next, offering a complete realignment of the human body and person."

After the 12 sessions of bodywork, I delved deeper into the conversational aspect of the work in Anne-Marie's Creative Leadership Coaching program. This coaching provided thought-provoking explorations into one's belief systems, language patterning, and listening skills. Through this, I improved my communication skills. We also dug even further into the root of my issues.

During these sessions, my commitment to writing my book came up. I really wanted to get this book going. Anne-Marie helped me set goals for the book. She said, "Listen: Get to work. What's the deadline?"

I said, "I want to get the first chapter done by this week."

And lo and behold, of course, I jumped right into it! I was physically there—I was aligned, doing breathwork, feeling stronger, practicing dance. I let Anne-Marie read one of my first drafts, and her feedback was inspiring.

When I walked into her office, I complained about my business and how my life seemed to be spiraling out of control. I was completely overwhelmed. I kept letting my injuries define my life and wellbeing. With all these things going on in my life, I felt like a one-woman show taking all duties in a three-ring circus. Of course, not limited to juggling flaming daggers, taming the lions, and tightrope walking all at the same time!

This dangerous and overwhelming train of thought wounded me! In turn, it derailed my body from the right tracks of recovery. Anne-Marie heals with love. She will accept you exactly as you are. She exudes unconditional love and concern when healing others. Anne-Marie showed me new methods of thinking and ripped the veil off of what I couldn't see because I was stuck in my old patterns of thinking. Today, I have great relationships with colleagues, balance my work schedule, prioritize my life, and embrace the constant motion that time brings upon us.

She changed my thought sequences and gave me techniques to move forward. These practices kept my motivation level up, helped my mind, and got the wheels in motion for me to move onward. Through Anne-Marie's help, I positively mapped out the route of my life.

Uniting the whole body, mind, and spirit enabled me to confront emotional issues that my health problems were causing. I was willing to explore the psycho-emotive components of the work and I acquired more freedom in my body and soul. I grew taller too!

People who do the sessions can actually grow from a one-quarter of an inch to a full inch. This is because they become much more aware of their postural alignment that works directly with what they are thinking.

Finally, I felt like my health and my life were under control. This was another great stepping stone in my step-by-step healing process. I still had more healing work on the horizon.

CHAPTER 9:

Rebuild/Rebirth

Henri and Anne-Marie first introduced me to breathing the right way. I loved how they helped me heal, and I felt how breathing improved my wellbeing, so I did more research.

I found out about high blood pressure specialist Dr. Larko. Through his extensive experience, Dr. Larko developed a system to read your blood pressure differently than most doctors do. He claimed that the top number in your blood pressure reading represents your emotional state and the bottom number is your blood flow. The top number changes depending on your feelings, while the bottom number stays the same. If you uncover what is going on in your psyche and naturally deal with the emotional issues in your life, your blood pressure will automatically lower.

I came across Leonard Orr in my research. He created "rebirthing," a form of breathwork that corrects your air-flowing patterns, controls your emotions, and realigns your thinking. Orr invented this method in the 1970s after experiencing his re-birth of sorts while taking a bath. Orr determined that through breath control, one could uncover suppressed trauma from childhood. Through this system, one can heal those wounds for a healthier lifestyle.

Through proper breathing, Orr believed that people can rid themselves of emotional burdens, alleviate pain, prevent disease, and avoid physical decay. With the help of a practitioner, you are taught techniques to help become a better breather and put yourself in a more heightened state of self-awareness than you've never achieved before. With this process, you can tap into the negative energies that you didn't even know existed. Releasing this harmful energy enables you to exhale out the negativity, thus propelling your physical and mental health into a state of liberation.

It was just about time for me to find a breathing mentor. Serendipitously, I was about to meet someone who specialized in this exact type of healing. Through a mutual friend, I was introduced to a rebirthing specialist named Bassam Younes. Rebirthing is a great technique to get to the root of your problems and mend your wounds. It is frequently included in people's spiritual practice to help them reach their overall goals.

Hailing from Lebanon, Bassam is a breathwork extraordinaire, who lives in Australia. During his travels, he always puts New York on his itinerary. I fortunately caught him during one of his Manhattan visits. Bassam is a highly spiritual individual who uses his intuition to help clients take a holistic approach to healing and self-discovery. He comes from a diverse background in both personal and professional realms. Raised in Lebanon in the 1970s, he longed to study Eastern and Western healing techniques. After participating in the fashion industry as a model, he became disheartened with the superficial world of glitz and glam and turned to meditation to repair his state of mind. Later, Bassam learned about breathwork and studied with the rebirthing chief himself, Leonard Orr.

Besides rebirthing, Bassam also specializes in astrology, meditation, and therapeutic sessions to help his clients unlock their unconscious selves. In his bio, he states, "The breath is my primary teacher! It is one of the four architects of universal creation. It will reveal to the willing the secret doorways to joy, purpose, and meaning." People walk around in their daily lives unaware they are carrying their own burdens. By not by coming to terms with these issues, you can damage yourself.

When you go back and relive your own birth in rebirthing, you heal the old wounds you thought had long since disappeared from your system. When these festering problems reappear through rebirthing, you release them. Like Bassam taught me, everything is cyclical. Things come, things go, and you just have to learn how to deal with them. Through these cycles, you need to release everything through breathing. This is crucial in unlocking your true nature to reach your full potential.

My rebirthing sessions with Bassam lasted one and a half hours each, and I did a total of 12 sessions. Bassam came to my apartment in New York and started each session by telling me to lie on sofa and start breathing. While focusing on the present moment, you visualize the air entering, circulating, and being released by your body. You have to clear your mind and focus all of your energy on relaxing and breathing. I became mesmerized with the sensations my body began to feel. I felt vitality boiling inside, tickling my veins with tinges of hot and cold. I kept on breathing and cleared my mind. While manifesting this energy, your body begins to let go of harmful vibes and life experiences that may have negatively affected you at a young age. It took me a little while to get the hang of just inhaling and meditating in the moment. After the sessions, the whole process became second nature to me.

Going back to my chapter on breathing, let's revisit the Taoist philosophy, rooted in Chinese beliefs and customs: how remembering your inner child and breathing like you did in the womb can help you tap into the problems that lie under your surface holding you back in the present. Only after rebirthing did I realize the effect that my premature birth had on my life. By revealing this state, I started reliving my youth!

Flashback to the day I was born. My mom gave birth to two identical twins, Robin and me. We were prematurely born at seven months, each weighing two and a half pounds. In the womb, we practically breathed each other's air. Because we were born too early, we both experienced our fair share of health concerns. For two and a half months, our lives were in jeopardy. Our health was so unstable that we had to live in an incubator. My sister experienced the bulk of the issues. Most of the medical attention was focused on her, leaving me in second place. When I did regression therapy once before rebirthing, I remember that I cried in the incubator and felt helpless because nobody paid attention to me. My sister was favored because of her conditions. These events made me want to compete for the first place spot my sister always held by default. At that point, I was literally stuck in the box, confined by my circumstances. I knew that it was in my future power to conjure my own way of life, making my own path to live by my terms.

When siblings are born close together in age, sometimes they feel like they are in competition for attention and care. Many children with siblings feel this way. My folks did the best they could to cope with these circumstances and wanted to accommodate both of us to lessen the competition later in childhood.

My sister maintained that attention as we grew, needing special exercises to improve her eyesight and such. Even though she was the only one who needed those exercises, my parents also did them with me, going above and beyond to treat us equally. We were treated on the same level, but for some reason, I still felt isolated.

Looking back, the family took very good care of me, yet I felt ignored and did anything I could to attract attention, going so far as banging my head on the pillow as a six-year-old. My parents finally took me to see a doctor. They held my sister's hand while I was dragged behind. When they asked the doctor why I was making such scenes, he told them it was perhaps because I felt threatened by the race for attention. In the fourth grade, I pretended my foot hurt and walked around the house with a cane, only to run down the block when nobody was looking. I thought that would *really* grab everyone's attention.

With Bassam's help during rebirthing, I realized my constricted breathing started during childhood, going back to the day I was born. As a premature baby, I came into this world gasping for air and struggling to breathe. Babies born before 36 weeks have undeveloped lungs. This can lead to many medical complications if they don't get enough oxygen. My sister and I spent the first months of our lives in an incubator with impaired breathing as the result of this situation.

The pent-up pain I had was all because I overlooked the simplicity of breath and never allowed myself to concentrate on such easy principles. Even when I was on top of the world as a bodybuilder, I was living for tomorrow, not in the present moment. Through breathing, I released the trauma I carried around from childhood.

My outlook on life started in that incubator box. I was constrained by circumstances out of my control, forcing me later in life to be an out-of-the-box person. The lack of immediate attention from my parents forced me to live my life in the grandest way possible, hoping to get noticed. This is why I'm an overachiever and feel the need to do everything to the umpteenth degree. I was always competing with my sister. And then, the competition turned into a one-woman-show where I competed with myself during my bodybuilding phase in the early-2000s, constantly pushing boundaries and limitations, not obeying my body. All of this kindled the fire underneath me to always go outside my comfort zone of safety and security. This approach periodically got me in trouble. My passion has helped me live a great life; however, my initial bodybuilding accident also occurred from my tendency to be amazing all the time. I wanted to be the strongest I could possibly be and I did not listen to my body when it showed signs of strain. With healing, I wanted to be better and pain-free, so I did everything to fix myself.

When I was first learning to breathe, I could not feel anything. I thought my coaches were out of their minds. I thought, "This is crazy! This is not working as well as I would like it to." I desperately wanted what they had—emotional freedom paving the way for physical freedom. One day, it clicked, and I got hooked. The breathing techniques I learned through dancing and rebirthing were actually helping. And these practices were actually fun! Even today, as I breathe in through my nose and out through my mouth, I imagine the air materializing before me and I live in the moment. I circulate the air through my body in a more mindful manner. We all have emotions from birth, and sometimes we don't even know what they are. The longer it takes to come to terms with them, the harder it is to let them go. It is within your power to release the tension and break free from destructive patterns.

We can all recognize a particular emotion, allow it to run its course, and let it go. Over the course of two weeks, I completed eleven rebirthing sessions and converted my negative emotions and energy blockages into positivity. The rebirthing sessions reconditioned me! I am now more confident and I feel more balanced. In fact, I'm still a big thinker, but not for the same reasons as before. I just think differently than most people do. I no longer harp on my past troubles because now I know that they do not define my future. Because I healed these past wounds, I am on my way to becoming personally fulfilled. And because I took control of myself in this powerful way, my blood pressure even lowered naturally. In addition, my friends noticed that I was calmer after rebirthing. I felt a difference in my speech and I was even thinking more clearly.

Rebirthing helped me gain a heightened sense of tranquility and clearness. I had a new beginning. Rebirthing enabled me to release things that did not serve me well. I also trusted Bassam in the process and learned through this willingness.

The breathing I now practice helps me gain more mobility and liberation, giving me the freedom to choose and live and the ability to overcome whatever curveballs life throws in my direction. This freedom leads to progressive motion, leaves no time for stagnation, and harbors positive energy that I can guide into future opportunities in my life's journey.

CHAPTER 10:

Moving Along with the Breath of Life and the Movement Man

No holistic approach to healing is complete without some yoga practice! I channeled my inner Mick Jagger though dance, and now it was time to become an enlightened bodhisattva. You know how Buddha was meditating under the Bodhi tree and stood up one day filled with a sudden understanding? Well, that's how I feel, still to this day, after my practices.

Now that I'm so used to my yoga practices, I've become the ultimate yogi. I can't imagine my weekly routine without yoga. I love yoga because it is an engaging form of meditation for the entire body. This type of movement and concentration enables me to stretch my body, mind, and spirit, enhancing my quest for physical, emotional, and psychological freedom. During these sessions, I stay in the present and drive my focus toward the things that only matter in the moment. Did I have a stressful day at work? Do I have to do 250 things before the sun sets that evening? I'm not thinking about these things. During yoga, I'm only concentrating on my connection with the body and my breath. Even when I do sometimes feel pain during sessions, I drive the focus to wherever it's tight and allow the pain to subside with each breath. Inhaling and exhaling is all that matters!

The trusty Anne-Marie Duchêne recommended yoga practice with Lola Rephann, who has been a great fit in my phenomenal lineup of superstar trainers. Lola has an interesting outlook on what she does, focusing on using yoga to mend the mind, body, and spirit. Lola's holistic approach is applied as a healing modality and as a tool for increased consciousness, mindfulness, and connection to the self. She's been a yogi for over 20 years. The yoga she currently practices draws from her extensive experience, including everything from Hatha Yoga, Forrest Yoga, and Yin Yoga, to meditation and Thai massage. Through her practice, much emphasis is placed on her intuitive understanding of people. While practicing yoga, I too find this particular correlation to be extremely important. Lola said, "The connection of how our mental and physical worlds are manifested in the rhythm of the physical body is vital."

Lola works with a diverse assortment of students. She said, "As a teacher, I work with individuals who come to me and say, 'I want to do this or that.' Some want flexibility, increased strength, stress management, and they might have tension or anxiety." I attended my first session with Lola wanting a little bit of all of these things, still keeping my recovery in mind.

The sessions with Lola overlapped with everything I absorbed under Anne-Marie's tutelage about the body's fascia through body-work and breathing. I was excited to learn how Lola also emphasizes breathing. She always said, "Debbie, you have to breathe into specific body parts." I thought this concept was absurd at first! But I started breathing into different body parts, such as my toes, my back, so on, and it was working. I established a circulatory airflow in my body and was on the path toward reaching my yogic goals.

After my first session with Lola, she was so inspirational that I deemed her, "The Breath of Life." She breathed life into my practice and helped me unlock my body's full potential. "I see things in my students," Lola said, "and we begin addressing these matters through the physical practice of yoga and breathing." She classifies breath as "a key indicator of what is going on in a person's inner world." According to Lola, the breath capacity, the ability to breathe completely, allows people to have a somatic experience of the breath in deep relation to the body. Having the capability to "feel where the breath is in your body is a precise way of discovering where the physical, mental, and emotional traumas lie within." Lola knows there is always more to an individual than what they report on the surface. Part of Lola's practice focuses on uncovering where unresolved issues lie in the body. Through this exploration, Lola's yoga practice helps to establish "a deeper integration." Lola helps me feel more present and self-aware. She picks up on "how people's life stories have been written on their bodies, minds, and spirits, increasing the person's sense of empowerment and overall wellbeing." Lola is someone who has used yoga for her own healing and mindfulness, and she fully understands the consciousness awareness that broadens one's path.

Another reason I love yoga with Lola is because the series of poses she teaches are challenging and rewarding. She mixes a combination of different methods. Here's a breakdown of my typical sessions with Lola, as told by "The Breath of Life" herself:

"We start with a series of Yin Yoga poses. They access the body's deeply held tensions in the fascia. In the yogic anatomy, the fascia is considered to be the emotional body where we hold all of our patterns, traumas, injuries, and memories. We open each session with some warm-up Yin Yoga work. Then we move into some Forrest Yoga, a very breath-based practice." She asks me to use my breath as the key tool of inquiry. You feel with the breath where the body is closed, resistant, or open, and you follow the breath into these areas. Core integration work is helpful for someone like me who should place emphasis on this area. Lola said that I have some energetic blockages where I need to wake the tissues that have been previously traumatized. The core work helps me feel where I am not feeling. This helps me know where to go with the breath and movements, clearing up how the breath, body, and emotional aspects are connected. I connect back to the places that were injured.

Next is Vinyasa work that is more alignment-oriented. It helps me connect to where I'm out of whack. Lola said, "By going into alignment, we find where we habitually need help. We can track that back to where we are disconnected, how we became that way, and which areas of the body overlay the chakra system. What the general themes or patterns we tend to move away from are exactly the areas we need to move toward." This approach of overlaying these different techniques works very well with me.

The finale of each session is so calming. We end class with a Thai massage that helps me relax. Because Thai massage works on the fascial level, it continues to help me heal and feel where the blockages are, where things are opening and closing.

The body's fascia is where our emotional issues are stored. Moving and breathing through whatever is stored in your body's fascia helps release any pent-up problems and emotions, thus enabling motion to occur. By practicing yoga that opened my fascia and increased my range of motion, I was freer and more mentally and physically advanced than I had ever been.

Lola helps me greatly. She is able to see where I am holding back and pushes me whenever I need to go further in my practice. Lola encourages me to feel more fully connected with the somatic experience of healing that can be accomplished on physical and emotional planes. She recognizes my desire for pain-free living and my persistence and said that I am "up for any challenge on all levels."

Lola herself has experienced healing on various levels, and she brings her own experience into her work. Lola said that when she first met me, we connected because of holistic healing principles. Lola's philosophy is simple: "When and where possible, just heal yourself." Lola only sees medical intervention, such as medication or surgery, as a "last ditch effort." She said, "There are reasons for surgical or medical interventions, but the holistic self-healing method is the first step to pursuing genuine healing." Lola is a truth-seeker in her yogic practices. "When people are avoiding the past," she observed, "they are not going to find true wellness." They are going to keep covering up and medicating away what really needs to be resolved at a greater level.

Since I've started Yoga, Lola has observed a shift in my overall demeanor and body. She saw how my body and mind have impressively opened up. I have become more aware of my breath and I recognize how attention to breathing is instrumental in healing and staying connected with myself. Lola knows how I truly want to heal and that I'm completely committed to the holistic path of wellbeing. Lola also believes that everything in my life is filled with an authentic representation of who I am. Lola said all these things have helped me get to where I am going, healing-wise and beyond.

After trying yoga, I scheduled appointments with Bill Hedberg, the bodywork specialist from Shen Tao Studio. The techniques at this training center combine various methods of movement to stretch the body. Bill prepares my body for dancing and enables me to reach my tip-top shape and potential. I refer to Bill as the "Magic Movement Man" because he miraculously stretches my body through bodywork.

Among his long list of specializations, Bill focuses on personal training, coaching, rehabilitation from injuries, and deep tissue bodywork. As a professional dancer and movement educator, Bill gets what I am going through. Bodywork uses deep pressure, gravity, and force to loosen the body. Bill manipulates my body, stretches, pulls, and twists out the pain. He targets the areas, such as specific muscles, tendons, and joints that need the most attention. Bill noticed that I usually arrive to each session in a tense state and in a fair amount of pain. But within the first 20-30 minutes, my body de-tenses itself and I begin seeing results. Shen Tao gives me a theory and understanding on how the body works. Each time I participate in bodywork, my body becomes freer, more flexible, and I feel more like a dancer.

For the first hour or two at Shen Tao, we work on a lot of stress and pain relief. I have extreme acupressure and vibration from the center's massage machines. Next, I get hooked up to what Bill calls the "torture devices." Here are some examples of the equipment I use with Bill during sessions: the ladder, swivel stand, rolling cart, weight track ladder, and calf stretcher. I do some bench-related exercises and other movements to combine stretching and strength training. It's as if Bill reveals magical powers through bodywork! Bill said that because I am so incredibly muscular from my weightlifting career, we try to pull the muscles forcefully into lengths, and then they are massaged at the same time. By the time the third hour of class rolls around, I complete most of the stretches and strength exercises myself under Bill's supervision.

Through this process, I am able to find emotional, spiritual, and physical freedom through movement. Bill explained, "Everything that is contracted hurts. The idea is that when muscles are tight, they hurt. When joints are jammed and pushed in like the glove compartment of your car with too many things inside, they hurt. How does bodywork help in recovery? At Shen Tao, we pull everything back out and make the muscles relax." When I engage in full body movement, the body's fascial system opens up and I feel better. In addition, I also feel long-term results. I feel fitter, stronger, and physically ready to take on anything!

Working with Bill at Shen Tao is basically a form of dance therapy. Bill explained how he prepares students for dancing: "You go into dance and you have the muscles in your thighs all cramped up. They are going to jam the lower leg into the upper leg, and the upper leg into the hip. If you try to dance, you're going to pull a muscle about 90 seconds into class. If you picture the ropes of a sailing ship and they're all tied up and snarled, you can't sail." Dancing without taking the right steps beforehand can be quite dangerous. I couldn't afford other injuries brought on by dance, so I always stretch before dance classes, as well as with Bill.

At Shen Tao, Bill builds my coordination and expands my form, given that I'm already pretty strong. Bill works on opening up the joints. Because I'm not 18, I can't get injured at this point! "The work here is to make sure that nothing gets pulled, ripped, or run down by pressure," Bill said.

I've drastically improved while working with Bill, and he agrees! He said, "Debra, you didn't get to your level of professional weightlifting by being gentle with yourself. You got there by abusing yourself very violently by tearing the muscles daily, overloading them by pumping iron." The greatest influence Shen Tao has had on me is that I've cut down on the violence between me, myself, and I. I can still go to my extremes with a gentler, less aggressive attitude. I've learned to take it easier. It is unnecessary to be in fierce competition with myself all the time.

One of Bill's metaphorical jokes in teaching is that we've changed the training technique from "shaking the baby" to "rocking the baby." He explained, "If we think of our muscles like a baby, we can shake them like a ridiculous human being that is being forceful with a child or we can change the rhythm and comfort the child. It's all in the attitude." I incorporate his sage advice while I move through life. Bill agrees that when we face potential failure with ourselves or ask ourselves to change, it is difficult. But once we decide that it is a decision-making process and we consciously choose to make the change, it is a step in the right direction of healing.

Bill pointed out how I can make the most progress. He encourages me to progressively believe in myself through each session. He said, "It doesn't really matter if we get there, wherever *there* really is in terms of end goals. What really matters is that we have set intentions and move toward goals." I couldn't agree more with this philosophy for healing and life.

Bill described the struggles that athletes, such as myself, encounter on a daily basis: "How hard should I push? If you push too hard, you'll break yourself. If you don't push hard enough, you'll cheat your potential. It's the great curiosity for human excellence. What's the balance between too hard and too soft? I think that's what you're trying to find. I think that's what we are all trying to find." I went so hardcore with everything in my life. He said I really experimented with "warrior energy," doing the strength and energy thing. I am still finding the opposite of that and working on a gentler approach to myself. These are all things we must tackle when moving to the next level in life whether at the gym, in the office, or walking down the street. When you learn to calm down, monitor your body's exertion, and tame yourself through controlled movement and breathing, everything else becomes more beautiful.

The bottom line is that motion means life, while immobility means death. This concept goes back to simple physics: A body in motion stays in motion, while a body at rest, stays at rest. We have to identify and strive for the healthy balance between work and play. It is within our power to choose how we use the kinesis we've been blessed with. We have the freedom to move and choose—whether it's dancing at home to your favorite song, walking to the store, or having an intense sweat session at the gym, you have to make these activities count in the long-term process of freeing yourself. Self-determination and freedom are enabled, helping you in your quest of growth, development, and healing.

Proper movement is key in living a happier and healthier life, all while softening your heart, opening up the body's fascia, and breaking down the issues within. Once you let yourself move, live, love, trust the process, and embrace the change that awaits you in all aspects of your life, you'll be freer. Trust me, it works.

CHAPTER 11:

Stem Cells and Magnets and Vitamins, Oh My!

Switching gears back to my issues, I had been dealing with ADHD since my youth and researched healing options that could lessen my ADHD symptoms all in one shot. One of my friends sought alternative treatments for a brain tumor and tried stem cell therapy with Stem Cell of America. This therapy can treat and prevent certain conditions. It builds up immunity in the body and elevates your overall health. Stem cells are taken from fetuses and gathered in an injectable form. These cells are inserted into the body and internally synthesized to promote healing. It can generate new cells and help strengthen the immune system.

Stem cell treatment seekers frequently suffer from conditions like autism, Alzheimer's, disease colitis, cerebral palsy, ADHD, leukemia, and cancer, just to name a few, and seek alternative treatment options. This therapy helped my friend, so I figured I'd give it a try to treat my ADHD. Stem cell therapy would help calm my active mind that came from ADHD.

I made sure to schedule an appointment as soon as possible because the office was far from home. A few weeks later, it was time for my treatment. I gleefully trekked to the facility, hoping for a cure. Several others and I had scheduled treatments on the same day, and we were picked up from our respective locations in a shuttle. Inside the bus, we all shared our stories of what brought us to treatment at Stem Cell of America. Their stories were inspiring, as they told of their conditions that ranged from mental difficulties to various types of cancer. I was the only one being treated for the first time, and each person on the bus sang the praises of stem cell therapy. Some of them had returned multiple times because of the stellar results. Some even visit Stem Cell of America every six months or so to upkeep their healing processes.

We all arrived at the office for treatment and were called one by one. When it was my turn, an IV was hooked into my wrist and one needle was placed in my stomach, alternating between four different spots. Success! From my other detoxes and several rounds of stem cell injections, these shots calmed my ADHD and my active mind that ran a mile a minute, going from thought to thought. These shots were golden to me! I asked the people there what makes these shots so special. They stated the cells do all the legwork once inside the body. I was so impressed with how the cells helped me!

I was metamorphosed. I blossomed like a caterpillar that turned into a beautiful butterfly and fluttered out into the scenic, sun-shining day. I felt awesome afterward, and I am still reaping the wonderful results of stem cell therapy.

I have been a happy patient of Stem Cell of America since 2008. After each treatment, I feel lighter and experience greater body and mind clarity. Because these treatments have worked wonders for me, I have since recommended them to close family friends, and they have benefitted from this therapy as well. I am so glad I tried stem cell therapy—it worked!

Shortly thereafter, several friends referred me to The Morrison Center for other alternative healing options. The folks there believe in the body's ability to instinctively heal. The talented team works to find the true cause of certain conditions and carves out a customized healing plan to encourage overall wellness in the body.

Dr. Morrison, the center's originator, takes a holistic approach to healing. His safe treatment plan helps prevent disease, cures health hurdles, and enables the body to reach its full potential. Dr. Morrison is board certified in family practice, integrative medicine, and is trained in environmental medicine. He is also a certified nutrition specialist.

I tried biomagnetism with Dr. Luis Garcia at The Morrison Center. Biomagnetism is a holistic therapy for healing, diagnosing, and preventing diseases. By placing magnets on the body in certain locations, many advantageous health effects can occur. Biomagnetism identifies the exact location of people's troublesome areas and works with the body to heal. Its health benefits include increased blood flow, oxygenation, and reduced inflammation, just to name a few. It restores natural health in the body by balancing pH levels. I was eager to try this therapy because it was another exotic approach to healing I hadn't yet tried.

Upon my first visit, I asked how many treatments I should have. He said around three or four treatments total. I was incredulous! With my other healers, they recommended 10 sessions or more!

I told him about my past injuries, and the general immobility on my left side. Dr. Garcia looked at my feet and diagnosed me accordingly. He told me things that were true about my health through muscle testing, a method of kinesiology. Dr. Garcia scanned my body from head to toe to identify issues. For the test, energy waves were sent through my body. As the scan reached my bladder, my legs shifted. Dr. Garcia saw this as a sign that represented bladder inflammation. Using the bathroom so frequently during the day and night irritated my bladder. From the scan, Dr. Garcia also said that I sometimes have a foggy brain, and biomagnetism could help me overcome this cerebral cloudiness.

Dr. Garcia placed North/South high field strength polarity magnets on my body. The time that each magnet stays on my body depends on the latitude in reference to the equator. At the equator, magnets are most stable. The further we are from the equator, the longer we have to wait for the magnets to work. Because I'm in NYC, the magnets stayed on my body for around 15-20 minutes.

I really liked the treatment and felt the miraculous effects of biomagnetism after just one session. When I walked in the office, my left toes weren't as mobile as my right ones, still as a result from my past issues. My toes felt very flexible when I left the office. After my session, my hands had less inflammation. Like my other healers, Dr. Garcia enabled movement in my body!

The Morrison Center's team also has a wonderful vitamin program. I learned about which supplements I should take for my toe situation and high blood pressure. I had taken many supplements in the past during my bodybuilding stint. The Morrison Center also advised taking various vitamins for healing.

Vitamin specialist Angela Young helped me select special vitamins. She said that it is crucial to take vitamins to increase energy to cells' mitochondria and maintain overall health. For muscular soreness, Angela recommended taking magnesium, a mineral critical to the body's overall health. Angela also advised on an immune boost supplement like buffered vitamin C and the vitamin RegeneMax with ch-OSA (choline-stabilized orthosilicic acid) and MSM 2000 for my toe issue.

Out of curiosity, I asked Angela what she recommends for high blood pressure and she said DioVasc from Xymogen works well. In addition, The Morrison Center also has a wonderful vitamin drip program. In the past, I've done hundreds of vitamin drips. I will try this in the future at The Morrison Center.

CHAPTER 12:

Using Oils

I started using oils back in 2012 when I met Paula, a natural health mentor. Paula and I convened at a course in New York City where she was reviewing the basic uses of oils. She taught me what essential oils are, how to use them, and why oils help the body. I soon learned that Paula was a certified oil practitioner. I spoke with her at length about my recovery progress. She told me to incorporate oils in my healing practice.

I started using high quality oils. These oils are extremely pure, concentrated, organic, beautiful, and of the highest vibration. They are made from plant essences, the oil distilled from plant matter.

Essential oils are the lifeblood of the plant, the liquid equivalent of blood in a human being. When using these oils, you're using the real deal! Humans are built to use plant-derived substances. This is why humans react well to plant essences.

How exactly are these oils derived? Imagine a cylinder about eight feet wide by 20 feet long that's filled with plant matter. Oils can come from the plant's bark, leaves, or petals. Various plants are used for essential oils. It is crucial for the plant matter to be grown organically, harvested properly, and placed in that cylinder. Water boils and when it reaches its boiling point, steam rises up. Oil and water do not mix. The steam pushes the water out of the plant matter. The water, called the hydrosol, is the plant's pure essential oil. It's very concentrated in this 820 plant matter-filled cylinder. One plant usually yields about 1/4 cup to 2 cups of distilled essential oil. These highly concentrated oils are of the purest quality!

Essential oils have medicinal purposes. Oils have anti-inflammatory effects on the body and have been essential for treating my injuries. These oils come in an assortment of varieties for specific needs. Humans have relied on plants for healing properties since the beginning of time. It is no wonder that plant oils have been used by countless generations to help heal!

When using essential oils, I apply them directly to my body or I ingest them. I learned about the different schools of thought for aromatherapy. America is usually more comfortable with the English model of aromatherapy. This method has come a long way from the time when essential oils were impure and diluted with synthetic additives. Essential oils used to come from inorganically harvested plants. In the English method, oils are always diluted and applied to the skin.

Contrary to the American system, I choose to follow the French and German models of aromatherapy. The French/German systems use small amounts of undiluted oils on the body, and you can occasionally ingest them. In certain cases, oils can be injected into the bloodstream too.

It's always interesting to learn which oils work well for particular conditions. For example, if you are using essential oils to treat a sinus infection, you can put oils in a diffuser to disperse essential molecules into the air. By inhaling the oils, you'll prevent infection in the sinuses. The oils will open the sinuses and drain them out. Most of us are familiar with Vicks Vapor Rub, a miracle when used on people with cold and flu symptoms. That was what most of our mothers used when we were kids. Vicks is just a synthetic version of essential oils.

For allergy relief or sinus problems, lavender, lemon, and peppermint essential oils come in a dropper to create powerful, all-natural remedies. I make sure to use these drops when I have seasonal allergies. To use, you put three drops behind each ear and behind the neck. Then, add five drops of each into an empty vegetable capsule and ingest it. You can also add one drop to a spoonful of honey for children. For adults, you can use two-three drops each. For earaches, you can place lavender or Helichrysum essential oils around the ear for relief three-five times a day until the pain subsides. Continue applying these once a day until the ears are completely clear.

Real essential oils give the body a very powerful feeling. When you're using essential oils for emotional balance, you can apply a balancing protocol called "Have a great day every day." First, I start with applying a blend called "Valor" that balances the body's alignment and electrical system. You apply this to the wrists. You then cross your wrists. This helps develop the left and right sides of the brain. They are very grounding to our energy levels. Very often, if we are anxious, our energy sits high up in the head like in the upper part of your body. When we apply Valor, it brings the energy down to the lower part of the body to makes us more grounded. With this, we can walk more firmly on earth in a calming way. You can also apply it to the bottom of the feet and just wait until you have calm feelings. It's very soothing.

The next part of that protocol is the oil called "Joy." It opens the heart chakra and uplifts the body. You apply it over the heart in a clockwise fashion to enable that warm heart-opening feeling.

The next part is called "Harmony." You apply this oil to balance all the body's chakras. When applying "Harmony," you'll have a very joyful experience. You give yourself a few drops on the solar plexus and rub it in a clockwise fashion to get charged with an ecstatic feeling.

The final part of the protocol is called "White Angelica," my personal favorite. It helps protect your field from negative energy. You apply it to your hands and rub them together. It also helps smooth your aura. You put some in your hair and on your shoulders. This oil is supposed to mimic the energy of having angels on your shoulders. It's like sprouting angel wings from your shoulders. It also balances your mood and lifts your spirits. You can do it several times a day.

Some oils can be adjusted to fix the body specifically. For instance, if I'm fighting an infection or if I feel really run down, I can adjust "Thieves" to suit my body's needs. "Thieves" is blend of cinnamon clove, lemon, and rosemary; it has very strong immune-supportive properties. I take it orally and sometimes drink it with tea throughout the day. I feel great when I use it. Compatible oils can also be mixed to heighten their functionality in the body. My young grandson also uses "Thieves" on his feet each day after his bath. He used to get to the second level of colds and sinus problems, but since he started using oils, his colds are less frequent. He is a healthier baby and doesn't miss any school days. I also use "Thieves" if I'm feeling run down or coming down with something. It helps me heal much quicker.

I can lower my high blood pressure using lavender oil. Many people have reported gradual lowering of their blood pressure when applying lavender and using a monitor. Because the left side of your body corresponds with the heart, you put a few drops of lavender on the left ring finger and massage it into your skin. You go down that whole body's heart channel, through the left finger, down into the hands, down the arm, to the middle of the arm, where the bicep meets the armpit, and up into the armpit. Massaging the heart channel helps your body. Then you lie down and relax. You can do this method as often as needed.

Frankincense is fantastic. I just love using Frankincense and enjoy how it works with my skin. Frankincense is one of the oldest medicines known to human beings. It supports the cerebral system, the neurological system, and the digestive system. You can also drink it. It helps with anxiety. A study was once performed on mice where their response to frankincense and anti-anxiety medication were tested. The oil was diffused into the mice's environment. It triggered a greater relaxation response than traditional anti-anxiety medication. I am always diffusing frankincense or applying it to my skin.

I love to spread the word that plants are here for us to use, especially for healing. This awareness has since taken hold in the world's collective consciousness, which is always wonderful to see. Oils can also help people come together to discuss the importance of wellbeing. It is great to gather communities or groups together to talk about it. To me, it is an ancient form. It is a return to how women really healed their children in olden times. Not that I think that doctors should be ignored—they have their place. But I think that we, as humans, have surrendered our power over our health and placed it in the authority of doctors. Using alternative methods is one way to take back the power of health. We can do so much more for ourselves, and we can share each other's experiences and affirm how we can empower ourselves. This is part of the planet's healing process and helps spark consciousness. I am glad I learned about all this through oils.

Here is a photo of my favorite oils:

CHAPTER 13:

Shaking It with the Rhythm Queen

Boom, bam, bop! Clap, clap, clap! Here comes the rhythm queen, Cecilia. She's dancing along to her own life's beat and grooving in style. From the moment she arrived at my door, I felt like I was in the presence of a queen. I watched her sizzling dance reels online and wanted to dance like her. I scheduled lessons per Anne-Marie's referral. With the moving essentials given to me by the fantastic Henri, this was the perfect next step in learning dance. Cecilia was actually Henri and Anne-Marie's dance teacher. I was honored to sharpen my tools with Cecilia while transforming my stiff body-builder form to that of a fluid dancer. Cecilia's World Jazz skills of rhythm and movement made me want to move like that too! Some people don't have rhythm or movement, so it's important to discover these skills. If you don't move, you lose your agility! It was now really clear that I wanted to be a dancer to stay healthy!

Since 2014 and beyond, I've been taking movement classes with Cecilia. Each session is diverse, inspiring, and rhythmically charged. I challenge Cecilia because I am still learning what it takes to feel the beat and move in time to it. She's never had a student like me before! Cecilia encourages me to listen to music, connect with it on a deep level, and get back to the instinctual nature of rhythm. We all have this rhythm inside us; we just have to activate it and practice. Cecilia wants me to pay attention to the instruments and identify each one. I love finding the bass line and bopping along to it! Music opens up the soul! Careful listening lets me feel the music even more when I'm dancing. I let my body synchronize to the tune and unleash my inner lion nature, raring and roaring on beat to the music. In class, we work on identifying each instrument independently and how the beats contribute to the song as a whole. We also clap out rhythms with our hands.

With movement, Cecilia helps me expand what she calls the "internal river" to set my life's groove and make me move. Awakening the internal river allows me to dance! My definition of the internal river consists of making my body softer, as opposed to the taut body-builder I once was. It gets my energy flowing, moves air through my body, and runs my body's river to the music's rhythm. This river is always there, but you need to recognize its presence to open it up. Think of it this way: We need to connect back to the fact that our bodies are made up of approximately 80% liquid. When you know the internal river is inside you, you'll be liberated and burst the river open in a queen-like style. I gain movement while focusing on my internal river. And Cecilia knows how I'm all about finding physical freedom with movement and dance.

After about a year into Cecilia's lessons, I had a jaw-dropping moment when I realized the first step in awakening the internal river. I was at the manicurist one afternoon when the radio played one of my favorite songs. I jumped up from the chair, set the metronome in my head to identify the rhythm, walked in time to the beat, and felt soft and sexy. When you connect to the music, your body relaxes. This was such an incredible feeling! I unleashed my movements and jazzed to the song. I was living through the music in that moment! I felt my heart, body, and soul healing! We should all feel this when recovering happily.

In class with Cecilia, we also focus on breathing. When she taught me this concept, she said: "When we are breathing properly, we are able to isolate the breath to different parts of the body. Then the body is loosened with breath." Airflow is life. Realizing this builds strength and confidence. Breathing wakes up my body and rejuvenates my muscles. Dancing like this is freeing, and makes me feel sexy. It's no wonder that Cecilia invented "cexci breath," [pronounced "sexy" breath] to get in touch with your inner nature. With this, I relax the tension in my mouth and concentrate on what's happening through the power of "cexci breath." When I first learned "sexy breathing," I stuck my tongue out to open my respiratory system. It wakes up the core, gets air into your chakras (energy points in the body), and invigorates the body. With acknowledging my chakras and breathing, I become more sensual and let go.

Here are explanations of each chakra and how they bring awareness to the body:

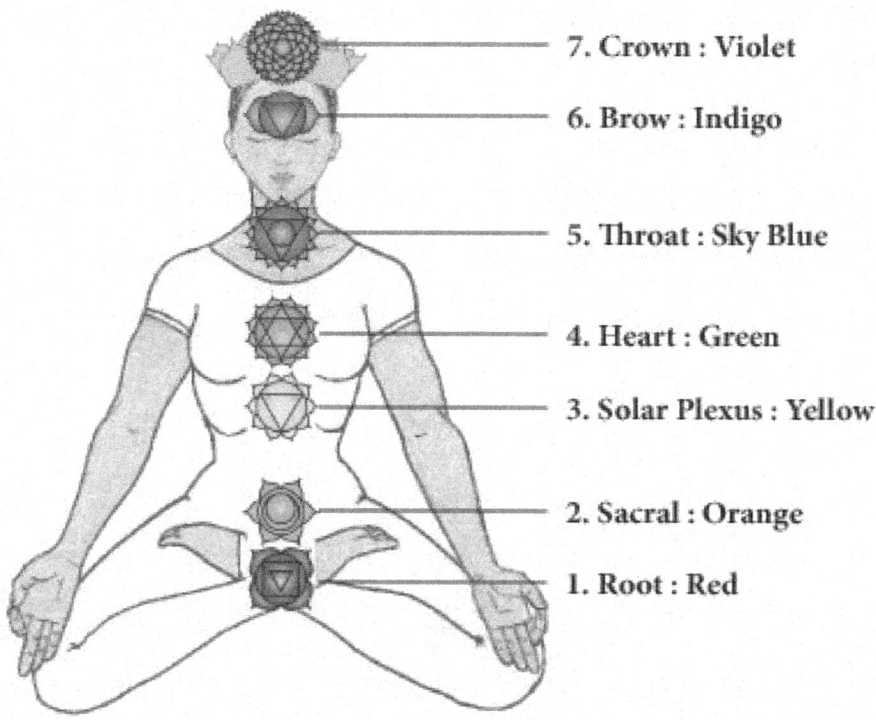

7. Crown : Violet

6. Brow : Indigo

5. Throat : Sky Blue

4. Heart : Green

3. Solar Plexus : Yellow

2. Sacral : Orange

1. Root : Red

The Crown chakra honors connectedness in the spiritual sense; the Third Eye (brow) represents your intuitive abilities; the Throat chakra signifies communication; the Heart chakra corresponds to the heart; the Solar Plexus chakra is the powerful life force; the Splenic (Sacral) chakra is your creative side; and the Root chakra respects the Earth and honors survival skills. I realize that these energy points help me heal and I activate them in movement class, engaging the whole body.

After warming up and focusing on my body's chakras, I can focus on core muscles with different poses, stretches, and repeated sequences. This practice also helps me strengthen my whole body's internal river flow. I love to do isolations and I perform several different ones each time. For example, we'll do a series of ribcage isolations, going side to side, then front to back.

Cecilia teaches my body to stretch. This enables muscle memory. I perform many stretches each class so I can move my body like a smooth snake, freely, in each way. These exercises get my body moving and become easier over time because my body can remember the movements.

When Cecilia is not dancing or working, she focuses on herself, takes care of her body, and celebrates all life's little moments, as do I. She embraces life as it comes and is as nimble as ever. She said, "Celebrate life, yourself, how you woke up this morning, and that you are here." Part of life's celebration comes from her rule of being kind to herself at all times and honoring the internal river. She said miracles happen when students trust in the process. You heal yourself on all levels with an open mind, body, and soul and have many "a-ha" moments along the way. I relate to this. Cecilia's useful tidbits and techniques helped me on my healing journey.

CHAPTER 14:

My Monumental Moments at Landmark

Another turning point in my healing journey was when I discovered Landmark, a personal and professional development center. Anne-Marie told me about this program, and I signed up straightaway. Landmark hit my life's gas pedal, accelerating me forward, so I could let go, with no braking in sight!

Landmark brought me back to my childhood and helped heal old wounds. I discovered how we all invent things about our existence when we are little. We carry these experiences with us and do not realize the impact they have on our adulthood. From certain things that happened to me as a child, I was stuck with a four-year-old mindset as an adult. From the thoughts of a toddler, I recreated my reality and believed every minute of it. At Landmark, I learned these stories were not real, and I let them go. I saw this as clear as my hand in front of my face!

I came to terms with the past and was ready to move forward with my life. Before I took the Landmark Forum, I had ridiculous thoughts in my head that dominated my life. The Landmark Forum took my past and left it where it belongs—behind me. It enabled me to have an optimistic future.

Throughout my life, I wanted to do my own thing. I was always motivated to be uniquely extravagant, and my personality was shaped by my family's dynamic and childhood experiences. As a teenager, I didn't want to listen to my parents' rules. They were very strict and did not let me participate in every activity I wanted. Many people have similar experiences as a teenager and think their parents' behavior is controlling and overprotective. Because my parents were like this, I always held a grudge against them and didn't like to listen. I told Landmark's share group about my familial experiences and the group's leader told me I was engaging with my parents through an "Already Always Listening" filter. It wasn't until the Forum Leader made this comment that I realized how my parents dearly loved me, always provided for me, and had my best interest in mind. They wanted me to be safe and responsible at all times. That is why they sheltered me. I learned to lift this filter and saw the tremendous love my parents exuded.

After my heartfelt share at Landmark, I called my parents and apologized. I told them how much I love them and what an honor it is to be their daughter. Today, I greatly respect my parents. We talk every day and they always listen to my life's stories. We are now closer than ever!

Landmark also provided me with the motivation I needed to get on the right path toward my life's goals. I was ready to take action! It pushed me further to get my book off the ground and made me realize my journey is ongoing. My first draft of *Happy Healing* sat on the shelf for four years, and I stopped myself from writing. I identified the internal thoughts and obstacles that got in the way of my passion for writing and helping others. I was once again inspired and nothing could stop me. I saw all possibilities in the world. After the forum, I started working on the book again, and I achieved my goals by making them happen.

Part of a secondary Landmark seminar I took in 2011 (I've taken many Landmark seminars focusing on different topics) was to design a project to benefit the greater good of society. I wanted to represent New York State's children and develop an act to empower them. I was inspired to change the law when my relatives were sexually abused as children by a person we thought we trusted. The pain felt by these children later was unbearable because the terrible acts affected them their whole lives. One person I knew suffered so much from the abuse that he took his own life. Children need to be taught in school about sexual abuse, report the inappropriate behavior, receive necessary support, and be protected by the law. It broke my heart to watch my loved ones suffer. So, I wanted to create a bill to speak on their behalf. It is terrible that the perverted abuser was not even convicted!

Taking action and protecting children by creating laws was the only thing I could do. I researched New York State's laws on child sexual abuse. There were some preexisting statutes in the process of getting passed, but I wanted to develop other bills to clarify what was already written. I drafted a version of a bill and called it The Precious Child Act, originally for Landmark's seminar. I told my mom about this project and she said, "You don't know anything about this topic. How are you going to do it?" I said, "I'm going to learn," and I started right away. Knowing me, I jumped headfirst into this project, researched everything I could about the legalities of this subject, and knew I would learn in the process. At this point, I wanted to make The Precious Child Act happen in reality and I desired to become a social activist, which was sparked by Landmark's seminar. I needed to make a difference in the lives of others and help the countless children of New York State whose voices are not heard. I started my first steps in propelling The Precious Child Act forward.

The Precious Child Act would prioritize safety. The current public school curriculum mandates instruction on child abduction, but does not teach children about sexual abuse. All children need to learn about these important topics. I learned about Erin Merryn's Law (A.90 Dinowitz/S.1947 Klein), an educational measure requiring schools to add age-appropriate education on sexual exploitation and abuse to the curriculum when teaching about safety and abduction. Children in grades kindergarten through eighth would benefit from this education. Bringing awareness to children about sexual abuse is empowering, enabling children to have resources available to them should unfortunate circumstances occur.

As part of The Precious Child Act, I wanted DNA samples of arrestees to automatically be taken when detained for certain crimes. I began making appointments with senators/assemblymen to spread my ideas. I needed senators to sponsor The Precious Child Act to address the urgency of this matter. After much time and effort, I sent letters to every senator and assemblyperson in New York State. I received meetings with three-quarters of the assemblypeople and senators in Albany, a great accomplishment for someone with no previous involvement in politics. I refused to take "no" as an answer! The Precious Child Act was becoming real! With my persistence, I made monthly trips to Albany to rally and meet with government officials. Now, everyone in Albany knows me! Senators expressed their tacit support of The Precious Child Act.

After many meetings, Senator Boyle agreed to write The Precious Child Act, Bill S5323-2015. This bill mandates felony arrestees to provide a DNA sample in connection to sex offenses where the child is younger than 13 years old. This bill was written exactly how I envisioned. It will amend the executive and criminal procedure laws. As of 2016, The Precious Child Act, Bill S5323-2015 is sitting in committee. I rallied in Albany on Feb. 24th, 2016 to draw attention to the cause, enabling the power of the people to help bring awareness and truly make a stand. The rally was a success! I also began supporting other pending bills pertaining to child sexual abuse: Senator Nozzolio's bill that raises the penalty for sexual abuse in the second degree from a class A misdemeanor to a class E felony, previously Senator Sampson's bill (S.4042 in 2015); Senator Nozzolio's other bill (A.2476 Englebright), establishing three new offenses of sexual assault against a child by a person in a position of trust, such as a person with responsibility for health, education, welfare, or supervision of a child for the subjection of a child, to have sexual contact by those people; Senator Boyle's bill (A.6961 Miller) that would require each public/charter school to post a child abuse hotline number in a readily accessible location for students; Erin Merryn's Law, (A.90 Dinowitz/S.1947 Klein), requiring schools to add age-appropriate education regarding sexual abuse; Senator Serino's bill (S.3696B) that would expand the single public lewdness provision to rename the provision public lewdness in the Fourth Degree.

The longer the government waits to pass The Precious Child Act and these other bills, the more liable its officials become. I cannot wait until these bills are passed. I will continue to advocate for children's rights and bring awareness to important causes through social activist work. Perhaps one day, I will continue my political engagement and run for senate.

Before I took the Landmark Forum, I saw life through a narrow four-inch filter. After the program, I saw life through a 100-foot filter! The whole world opened up for me and I saw the entire universe of possibilities, including activism, authorship, and more! It helped me follow my dreams. I visualized what would occur to make it happen and how to not take "no" as an answer in any aspect of my life. The lessons I learned at Landmark were invaluable. The forum enabled me to see each and every opportunity. I realized that with my willpower I could do anything in the world! Anything and everything is possible. It is in your power to design your own life! Nothing can stop you! I was ready to live life to the fullest and develop the following mantra; "Ready, world? Here comes Debra!"

CHAPTER 15:

The Icing on the Cake

In 2014, I attended The Mind Body Spirit Expo in NYC. I arrived and scoured the room filled with talented people and attendees. Within five minutes of entering the building, a man bolted seemingly out of nowhere and stopped me in my tracks. It was as if he teleported himself in front of me from another dimension. He came so close to me that I could practically feel his breath. He stood four inches away from my face and gleefully exclaimed, "$99! I CAN HEAL YOU."

I was like, "Woah!"

"I'M GRAND MASTER QI. I'M GRAND MASTER QI," he proudly broadcasted. I knew that Master Qi had something important to tell me. I realized he knew something I didn't know. I felt his force was one I needed to listen to. He had this staggering energy level, unlike anyone I had ever met before. He was operating on a whole other level, in an entirely different and bombastic universe.

Master Qi seemed crazy in the best possible way. I liked his energy and was drawn to him. I needed to learn more. I wanted his energy level. There was something so unique about this man. There was a glimmer in his eye that I had never seen before in any other individual. I was about to find out just what the *special* something was.

With the barrage of questions I suddenly had and the initial language barrier I encountered, I had more info to find out. I said I'd walk around the expo and come back. I found Naina, who ran the fair, and was told that Master Qi is a well-known international energy healer. He uses Qi to heal people. With the words *energy* and *healer*, I was in and ready to work with this man. So I marched back over to his table, and he said again, "I can fix you." We sat down and he listened to my pulse. By feeling my arm, he said, "Many things happened to you in the past. There are many toxins in your body. You've taken a lot of pills. Your back and neck were hurt. You have a bad stomach and high blood pressure."

I was amazed how he knew all of these things about me! I was shocked that he identified the exact sources of pain in my body. He continued with his diagnosis, saying that I was in an unbalanced state and that he could restore the balance in my life with energy. I soon realized that he was intuitive and gifted.

How could he have known this information about my health and me? Mind reading? Magic? Was he receiving messages from the divinities? Did I meet him before that day without even knowing it?

I told Master Qi that he was correct about all my ailments and that I had been on pills for four years. At that point, I had been taking vitamin drops from other healers for two years, and they weren't doing anything for my conditions. I hoped in my heart of hearts that he could help me. And I trusted that this healer could offer me something different to help me.

Master Qi kept saying, "Don't worry. Be happy." I was enamored with his positivity and liveliness! We exchanged information and I scheduled an appointment. I saw him at the fair on Friday, and by the early hours of Monday morning, I was trekking to his center in Flushing for a session.

That Monday morning was a turning point. I knew that another chapter of my healing path was opening before me. Fate had brought me to meet Master Qi. Hailing from China, Master Qi Feilong is a Qigong healer or energy healer. Isn't it bizarre that his name is literally Qi?!? I have wondered for sometime if he changed his name to Qi because he feels that he was just *such* a master.

In terms of "aura-talk," I know that mine's a vivid shade of red, but his read like burning fire. His was more than likely off the charts. I was practically lit on fire by his aura. It was so bright that I'm sure it wouldn't even fit on the spectrum because of its extremity. If you ever meet him in person, I'm sure you'd feel that strong presence too.

I bet you're wondering what the term "Qi" means, as I was the first time I heard the word. Qi, or chi (pronounced like "chee"), is the energy circulating life force whose existence is essential in Chinese medicine and its philosophic principles. Qigong is integral to Chinese practices to align the body, mind, and spirit. In Chinese culture, everything and everyone is connected through the vital energy force of Qi. Qi also has great philosophical implications. According to the Chinese philosopher Mencius, when Qi is harnessed appropriately, it can increase moral abilities and stretch to encompass the universe as a whole.

Another philosopher, Zhuangzi, once stated, "Human beings are born from the accumulation of *qi*. When it accumulates there is life. When it dissipates there is death... There is one *qi* that connects and pervades everything in the world." From Master Qi's swirling of energy and transmission of fascinating vibes, these ideas are exactly how I feel when I work with him. Since I've been graced with his resonating presence, I've felt more connected to the surrounding world and myself. Everything is clearer, brighter, and happier. It is no wonder that his catchphrase is the Bobby McFerrin/Bob Marley-style motto, "Don't worry. Be happy."

I arrived at his ornately decorated home office and was impressed with the many framed awards and diplomas that lined the walls. The photos of people he had met and helped glowed at me from behind the glass frames, grinning from ear to ear. I took my shoes off, as per Master Qi's directive, and entered his main energy-practicing room. Strangely enough, I felt better already! He gave me a tour of his mementos and was most excited about his Buddhist shrine that was lined with approximately 100 Buddha figures made from various stones. There was even a five-foot-tall laughing Buddha that was so splendid I wished I had one in my apartment.

I was served tea, and we sat down for the session. He told me an abbreviated version of his life story: Master Qi's parents were into Traditional Chinese Medicine (TCM). As a result, he was exposed to Buddhism from an early age. Because of his potential, he left home at seven years old. Master Qi's parents knew that he was special, so he was brought to the most prestigious Shaolin Temple. Located in the Chinese village of Zhengzhou, this temple (originated in 495 A.D.) was created to train the most talented in all the land. When Master Qi arrived at the Shaolin Temple, he received intensive one-on-one training with one of the best, Master SuYun. At the Shaolin Temple, Master Qi was taught Buddhist practices and principles, martial arts, meditation techniques, and other qi exercises. Average people couldn't possibly tolerate the discipline and rigor endured at this temple. Master Qi prevailed because he's *anything* but average. Master Qi suffered from illnesses when he was little and was cured by Shaolin Temple's headmaster, Master Su Xi. Master Qi harbors ancient wisdom from his learning at the Shaolin Temple and he supplements with additional lessons he has gathered along life's way. His beginnings at the temple honed his "skill set" for future healing missions.

Since Master Qi's beginnings at the Shaolin Temple, he earned many achievements besides energy healer and meditation master. He was a Qigong master, a Chinese medicine consultant, master of the 31st Generation of the JinGang One Finger stand in meditation, a ninth-degree black belt from the International Kung Fu Federation, international medicinal demonstrator and lecturer, and the most important title of all, as I refer to him, "The Icing on the Cake." This alias is because his method has greatly affected my already remarkable "cake" of healing and wellness.

Master Qi is a man, a myth, and a legend in his own mind. I think he's incredible. There are many "energy masters" in the world, but I can assure you that none of them is as original as Master Qi. He considers what he does to be a form of healing. The body generates a sustainable amount of energy used to complete many tasks that range from simple to complex. In our daily lives, blockages develop in our body. These obstructions can be caused from the toxins that we are exposed to, any negativity that surrounds us, and bodily injuries. We need to find a way around these blockages and gain more positive energy.

Master Qi has an interesting track record where he used his power and instinct for the greater good. He told me of the many sick people he treated, suffering from various health issues, and how he helped them recuperate. For this recovery, he harnesses new energy to clear people's stagnant energy. This stagnant energy is motionless and no longer serves a purpose to your body. Once this energy is cleared, the body generates fresh energy and your metabolism increases. This allows the body to cure itself and remove the blockages that were once holding you back. It makes you feel as good as new. According to Master Qi, I had many blockages caused from toxins in my daily life and from my pains of the past.

The first time I had a session with Master Qi, he asked me to write two words down on a piece of paper, fold them up, and hold them in my hands. He was going to try to guess the words. While he left me alone in the room and waited outside, I wrote two of my favorite words to represent my life: peace and love. He returned to the room and guessed my words! At that moment, I knew that Master Qi was so special! How could he have read my mind? His talents and clairvoyance enabled him to do so. I became inspired by this session and bought this amazing Chinese character to hang in my room, reminding me of my favorite word:

Afterward, he told me personal information about myself that nobody else would have known about, topics I had never told anybody before. Master Qi told me these things, and discussing them really helped with my detox, allowing me to further realize the burdens I was still carrying from past wounds. I wondered how he knew these ideas, and it is because we shared a special connection. Master Qi believes that we were brought together by fate and that our extraordinary bond stems from a past life. When I press him on the topic, he says that he cannot tell me fully because it is, in his words, "too complicated." I, too, feel like I may have known him from a past life. This greatly intrigues me because we both feel this immense connection. I'm a huge believer that we can recall our past life experiences.

In 2005, I had a past life regression session with a psychotherapist. Through this, I heard my cries in the incubator after my birth and recalled other memories. With this therapy, I learned about experiences I had endured over the years and carried with me.

Earlier experiences can trigger current emotions and open old wounds. Do you even wonder why you are inclined to like certain activities, people, places, or memories? Have you ever mastered something you've never done before on the first try? These memories could be from a past life. Another example of this is how I can use chopsticks perfectly. The first time I picked them up, I instinctively knew how to use them.

Another time I felt my past life memory kicking in was when I went canoeing down the Green River in Utah/Colorado, and I was amazed how comfortable I felt while canoeing. It felt like I had done it before. It was a surreal feeling! I've had several experiences like this in my life, and I believe this is knowledge from past lives.

In regression therapy, patients relive what has been forgotten in the past and dial into the subconscious mind. It releases what's hurting within, heals the psyche, and reboots your life's positivity.

Our personality and temperament are shaped by these long forgotten experiences. It is only when we come to terms with the past that we can recover and move on. Our character traits can change when we realize how they developed in the past with this therapy. Here's an example of how regression therapy helped me: Cleaning always made me angry and I never knew why. Through regression therapy, I learned I was a home-helper in ancient times that cleaned homes. I remembered being angry in the past and acknowledged why cleaning made me angry in my present life. I equated that task with stress that made me angry. After regression therapy, I no longer felt angry when cleaning. It was such a relief to determine why I felt like this.

Reliving the past helps us understand why we hold onto experiences and it heals us! Perhaps being graced by the familiar presence of Master Qi is a healing tool in and of itself! It was interesting to revisit the topic of past lives with Master Qi.

During my first session with Master Qi, we did several energy exercises to facilitate energy, healing, and detoxing. It was time for the highly anticipated foil detox. Before he started, Master Qi explained that extraordinary people have "lucky moles." I was informed that my lucky mole rested right on the side of my ribcage. Before the foil detox, I curiously inspected that area. To my surprise, sure enough, the mole was there, prominent and protruding!

Next, Master Qi explained that by placing foil on my stomach, my body would release toxins. He placed a piece of "regular" aluminum foil on top of my stomach and told me it was going to get hot. Master Qi stood back, flailed his arms, chanted in his native tongue, gestured fiercely, and performed his guru dance. He looked like a dragon getting ready for takeoff. Suddenly, searing heat hit my midsection. It felt like a hot pot was on my stomach. He picked it up and placed it down several times so it wouldn't get too hot. He peeled the foil from my stomach, picked it up, and held it up to the light. Many millimeter-sized holes appeared on the foil. A fine layer of gray soot lined my stomach like embers from a fire that had just gone out.

After the foil detox was over, he bolted from the room, sprinted to the bathroom in a fit of coughs and gagged. I was bewildered! I thought to myself, "What in the world is going on?" His interpreter told me that each time he does a detox, he needs to release the bad energy from his body that came from the person he healed. He eliminates from his body all energy that he extracted from your system. This way, your energy does not take away from his practice or drain his ability. He wiped the ashes from my abdominal area and told me I should feel healthier, and I felt better. Mission accomplished with the detox!

After detox treatments, my feet felt like they were planted on the billowy surface of clouds. I felt ethereal. My steps were lighter and my body was more flexible. I was looser and my legs walked with ease. Greater movement in my body was enabled! My energy level was higher, I was happier, and I had a heightened sense of bodily freedom. Master Qi brought out my youthful nature. "These detoxes—WOW," I thought to myself. I left Master Qi's office as a new woman, looking forward to my next detox sessions.

When I first started working with Master Qi, I thought, "This is crazy, maybe I should try something else." But something inside of me said, "Debbie, you've got to keep doing it." And I am so glad that I did because this practice has worked wonders.

Master Qi's philosophy on medicine and healing mirrors my own. He emphasizes healing and healthy living, and he appreciates alternate ways of curing the body and psyche. For example, he led his own holistic healing path firsthand at the Shaolin Temple, and he still meditates to maintain his health.

The "detox" he performs allows yin and yang to be restored in the body. To recharge from the detox, Master Qi meditates. As explained to me by Master Qi, yin and yang forces are the supreme forms of qi. They represent opposites that actually correspond to one another, making everything interconnected. These terms are interchangeably used in Chinese astrology to understand life. Master Qi calls on yin and yang to restore his energy and circulate the energy through the body. It makes him feel young again.

Yin represents femininity, the moon, and concealment. Yang represents masculinity, activity, openness, and the sun. Yin and yang always balance each other out. Its likeness is derived from its differences. One will reach a high state while the other is low and vice versa. These forces transform each other and bring forward a state of wholeness.

We all need energy to live, breathe, function, and survive in the real world, but compared to non-energy healers, Master Qi needs about 100 times more energy and focuses on yin and yang. In order to maintain this energy, Master Qi meditates each day anywhere from two to four hours. These meditation sessions are like plugging electronics into a wall and charging them. After meditating, Master Qi is ready to go and help the world! One of my goals is to be an energy master myself and to implement meditation practice into my daily regimen.

Many healers improved the color of my hands, but with this treatment, a lively color was restored. They are now a beautiful, normal shade. Most importantly, with the addition of qi in my life, I feel more connected to the world and myself. He has also enabled hand mobility through Baoding balls. I run these balls over my fingers and carry them in my hands a few times a week for 15 minutes. They help me relax and infuse energy to be dispersed throughout my busy day.

Together, Master Qi and I are a dynamic duo. When bright aura colors collide, magical things manifest, high-energy frequencies come together, and everything increases steeply to new levels.

CHAPTER 16:

Layering the Healing Cake

I saw Master Qi on a weekly basis for treatments. Master Qi's intuitive nature enables him to pinpoint people's pain and heal them in a loving way and balance their lives with energy. Working with Master Qi has been an extraordinary experience. With every treatment, I feel more alive and have more pure joy in my life. From the moment you enter his wellness center, you feel the love emanating from the walls and trickling down from the ceiling. The zen level of comfort I feel with Master Qi is unbelievable. The pageantry of taking off my shoes and drinking tea prior to the treatment preps me for euphoria and relaxation.

A typical visit to Master Qi's wellness center allows me to practice different techniques. After drinking tea, I lie down on a massage bed for 30 minutes. This makes me relax and concentrate on my body's airflow. I feel more energized after lying down and breathing. Next, I get a foil detox that is followed by cupping; cups are placed on my back and my body is detoxed. When I first started cupping, the round circles left by the cups were dark brown. Now the color is very pale. I feel the toxins pouring out of my body.

When I leave Master Qi's office, I feel this beautiful, clean energy. I am so grateful to work with Master Qi. In my eyes, he is a strong and gentle legend. There is balance between energy and stillness in his life that I have never seen before in any other person.

Master Qi also demonstrates at expositions and seminars around the world. The extraordinary talents that Master Qi performs range from energy dances, to slicing eight chopsticks in half with a $20 bill all at one time. He also jabs chopsticks in his neck and breaks them with his throat. He suspends bicycles with his teeth. Master Qi likes to light newspaper on fire, using the world's energy to set it ablaze. With this practice, he brings positive energy and warmth into the world. To stimulate brain activity and promote memory function, he does an exercise that involves slapping your elbows with your hands and then tapping your back. This is great to jog your memory and increase brain cell production.

Master Qi informed me that he was going to perform these talents on 2015's season of *America's Got Talent*, and he moved forward to the second round. I think the judges were so confused about what an energy healer was and they instead thought he was some sort of magician. During his first appearance on *America's Got Talent*, Master Qi was kicked in the balls by the host, Nick Cannon. How did he perform such a painful feat without feeling any pain? He controlled his energy to prevent himself from feeling anything. After his first appearance on this show, he was then invited to *America's Got Talent* in France to perform the same activities for a different audience.

I gladly accepted the invitation to watch him perform during NYC's audition round in 2015. I was floored! He captured the minds of viewers. I was so proud of him! After his wonderful audition on *America's Got Talent*, Master Qi pulled a long streamer out of his bag of tricks to symbolize energy and performed what he calls the "Dragon Dance." Everyone gathered around and chanted his name, enthralled with the energy he was emitting. Master Qi performs the "Dragon Dance" every day to garner energy and to relax his mind. I wanted to learn dances like this so I could become freer and synchronized with the energy around me.

Master Qi taught me special dances and movements like the "Dragon Dance" to trigger restoration in the body. He advised me to perform these dances each day. These movements build up immunity in the body, stimulate my body's cells, and enable my breath to flow like the wind. They're like caffeine to me. Starting off with one of these dances + drinking green and berry juices = the best days ever! These dances are crazy, wild, and filled with bizarre full-body movements to swirl energy in a confident manner. These dances were so unusual, but I did them anyway and trusted that they'd work. I knew they would pay off in the long run. Afterward, I always feel a natural high, a heightened sense of happiness, and my heart feels warmer. Master Qi told me to say the affirmative phrase, "Happy Happy Younger," when doing these dances. I feel freer and calmer, ready to take on each day with zeal! These dances reconfirm the simplicity of life for me. I've also taught these dances to my grandson. He's taken a liking to them and chants them non-stop. Because my grandson loved the dance so much, I realized I should teach the technique to more kids. In November 2015, I taught a series of energy dance seminars to my grandson's class at school. Kids have such great energy and view the present world as most important! I love sharing the knowledge of what I've learned on my healing journey.

Here's a photo of Master Qi and I doing the Dragon Dance:

The energy dances help me hone my breathing skills and move the air deeper through my chest, into my stomach, and down to my feet. Since I've learned so much from Master Qi, I've begun calling him "Grand Master." He has earned this title. I am grateful that Grand Master Qi taught me the Dragon Dance, which has been one of my favorites so far. When picking out my dragon streamer, I selected the one whose colors spoke to me the most, the dragon all decked out in bright yellow and green. This dance is healing, relaxing to the soul, and a very therapeutic activity. Dancing with the dragon calms my mind. It's amazing that you feel at one with the dragon. I listen to Chinese music while I fly it and allow my mind to be tranquil. You must always fly the dragon in a relaxed state. The dance brings positive energy into the universe, making the world a happier place, bringing joy to people. Since I started doing the Dragon Dance, I've made so much progress. Sometimes I feel that I am the dragon. I fly it higher with more loops and bounds each time. I'm starting to learn tricks, like a double-loop-run-through where you prance through the streamer on a whim. It feels like a circus trick. I always bring the dragon with me everywhere because the dance is so much fun!

When I travel to Florida on a monthly basis, I hold an energy dance meet up at the beach where the Dragon Dance is featured. I taught groups of all ages and the dance was well received, as beach-goers lined up to watch me and then try it. One of the people who attended my event stayed after the class was over to tell me how wonderful she felt afterwards, how she reached such a calm state of mind after doing the dance. I could see she was glowing!

One day in Florida after my meet up on the beach, I had extra time to practice the Dragon Dance. A group of children and parents gathered around, awestricken with my performance. They inquired, "Are you from the Chinese circus? The circus is in town!" I said, "Really?!? That's so funny! Do I look Chinese?" We all had a good laugh about it. It was so hilarious! Maybe one day I will pack up and perform my energy dances across the country on tour, as part of my own sort of traveling extravaganza.

The Dragon Dance brings me energy and joy! Happiness helps you heal. When you are happy, all negative energy bounces off of you. It does not get absorbed into the body. Positivity will take over and add to the happiness! Happiness is only for people who appreciate it. Make sure to surround yourself with positive people! Light attracts light! Positive energy attracts positivity! You get a natural high from happiness when you surround yourself with positive people. They uplift you and make your spirits bright. I am so addicted to this dance that I do it twice or more per day, flying it in the park, by the water, or in a vacant parking lot. I can't wait to run out the door every morning and do the Dragon Dance again. Just even thinking about the dance makes me excited. I think it's so incredible that I'm now better at the Dragon Dance than Grand Master Qi! I practice way more than he does and it shows. When I do the Dragon Dance, I feel like a phoenix rising from the ashes. Grand Master Qi once called me a phoenix and said that he is a dragon. I definitely identify with the phoenix.

Before working with Grand Master Qi, I couldn't feel the airflow going upward through my body. Now, with all of the breathing practice I've had through my other healing activities and with Grand Master Qi, I can literally feel the breath circulating through my body! It's astonishing!

Every year, Master Qi choreographs a new dance to coincide with the Chinese zodiac to represent energy healing and a target mindset during the year. These dances also protect the body, mind, and soul while expelling anything that would interfere with his Bob Marley-esque "Don't worry, be happy" outlook on life.

Master Qi practiced acupressure on me. There is energy in each pressure point that is manipulated through pressure. My body's pressure points are activated to maintain positive energy and clear any blockages that may have occurred. So far, he has activated pressure points on my back, shoulder blades, legs, and feet. I have actually felt the difference in my body from this technique. The blockages in my body are clearing successfully!

Besides helping me with his energy, Master Qi also recommended various tinctures and herbs to supplement the detoxes and acupressure. I'm going through menopause and it's natural for my body to change in this stage of my life. From my hormonal changes, I was suffering from low energy and extreme hot flashes. One minute,

I'd be fine. The next, it felt like I was lit on fire. When I started treatment with Master Qi, he recommended various herb tinctures to tame the hot flashes. I've felt an overall shift in my body, and my menopausal symptoms no longer exist.

Here are some of the supplements that I take under Master Qi's tutelage:

I've gotten hooked on dandelion tea, straight from Xinjiang's Kunlun Mountains in the northwest region of China. This bulk tea is so pretty because it looks like flower petals! It balances the system, detoxes the body, aides with digestion, rejuvenates, and purifies the blood. This tea clears the body of harmful toxins, bacteria, and viruses. Dandelion tea clears the skin! My face has never looked more radiant as is does now! This tea's vitamins and minerals are crucial to the body, including vitamins A, B, C, D, E, magnesium, calcium, iron, manganese, copper, choline, boron, and potassium. Dandelion tea reduces cholesterol, addresses flares in cases of hepatitis, and aids with muscular density. I drink over a liter of this tea per day. I have also increased my intake because it is so delicious (and great for my health)!

Master Qi takes mixed/crushed herbs and places them in medicinal black balls that I take each day. The most important is cordyceps, a mushroom in the fungi family that lives on caterpillars in the mountainous regions of Asia. The cordyceps that Master Qi gets are from Tibet. They are harvested in a special black soil enriched with special nutrients. The consumption of cordyceps is crucial to the Taoist principle called the "Three Jewels." These keystones of Chinese medicinal practice break down into Jing, Qi, and Shen; they are vital to the energies sustained in human life. Ingesting cordyceps caters to the Jing and Shen aspects of these principles. Jing represents the nutritive essence that is extracted and perfected and represents sowing the seeds of life. Shen means the mind, spirit, soul, and godliness embodied in deities. When you take cordyceps as a dietary supplement, you are becoming more united with the universe.

Cordyceps improves cold symptoms, like coughing, respiratory issues, and sinusitis. It also helps fight anemia, kidney dysfunctions, dizziness, weakness, and liver problems, and it balances cholesterol levels. Cordyceps helps reduce the size of tumors that could be associated with lung and skin cancers. For people with a variety of wide-ranging issues, cordyceps is an overall tonic and improves liver function.

Cordyceps can also be used as a stimulant, like coffee, to increase overall energy levels and endurance and reduce drowsiness. Master Qi swears by these fungi, and I have been taking them every day so I too can be one with the Jing and Shen aspects of Chinese medicinal practices.

Ginseng, the root, rejuvenates the immune system and has innumerable benefits. Taking ginseng improves concentration and mental performance, it limits fatigue and is a mood enhancer. This root fights heart disease, hepatitis C, and high blood pressure.

Master Qi has framed 20-year-old ginseng roots from China. He proudly displays them in his office. The ginseng was grown on the Changbai Mountain range. The newer ginseng he gave me took the form of a fine, raw powder, and was put in the black balls. I still take these as daily supplements.

Ginkgo biloba leaves come from a tree that helps improve brain function and memory. It speeds up blood flow to the brain and these leaves are received as an antioxidant by the body. Taking ginkgo biloba has eased my aches and pains.

Upon asking Master Qi what it is like to work with me, he said that I am a "super-genius" and he thinks my heart is "of the purest kind." He realizes that I have the ability to absorb his energy and said, "Debbie, not all people have the ability to do so! Some people resist it." He knows that in the future we could work together to make people understand how they too can heal from his energy.

Master Qi also noted that since I started working with him, I look 20 years younger and my energy level has improved!

Master of the Mind:

Since I started working with Master Qi, I began to feel significantly better! His sage advice is the best! Master Qi told me to become a master of my mind, not a slave to it. Buddha once stated, "To enjoy good health, to bring happiness to one's own family, to bring peace to all, one must first discipline and control one's own mind." So accurate! These principles are important when evolving into the best version of yourself. Becoming a master of the mind takes time. We will advance when we're kind to ourselves. Be in charge of what is going on in your mind and keep it simple. Do not overanalyze things and make them what they are not. Focus on reality. Empower yourself, be your own guru, and you can do whatever your heart desires. This opens up the world, and possibilities are endless. Our mind is our most powerful muscle, and we must exercise it in the right way! I am still working on this, as we all are. My mind-mastering abilities are becoming stronger each day by creating optimistic affirmations for optimal life performance. It is important to continue the process of re-training your brain for model mind mastery.

Here are some tips on being a master of the mind:

1. Meditate: Surprise! My favorite thing! Take time each day to appreciate life as it is. Clear your mind and enjoy yourself through meditation.
2. Think positively: Eliminate your self-defeating thoughts by re-equipping your brain to be optimistic. Confident thinking becomes easier with meditation.
3. Make yourself happy and laugh: Realize that nobody but you is in charge of your own happiness! It is in your power to make your own happy ending. Find joy and laughter in life's simplest moments. This is important to remember.
4. Focus on what you have, rather than what you don't: Always be positive and maintain a lovely outlook. Keep on smiling!

5. Make reasonable objectives: Set some goals you'd like to accomplish and make them happen. Skies the limit, but keep your feet firmly planted on the ground.

6. Read and write: Try keeping a journal each day and track your personal progress. This will psychologically help you. Read many books and stay inspired.

7. Take time for yourself away from your desk and electronics: Unplug and relax from time to time. Go take a walk in between bursts of work. Don't look at your phone before you go to sleep. You need time to recuperate away from your favorite gadgets.

8. Pick up hobbies to take focus away from your own mind: Take a run, go shopping, or learn a new skill. New things train our brain and boost our neuron transmissions.

9. Accept yourself and others for who they are: Know that you can't change anyone, and don't take things personally.

10. Let it go: Trust in the process and let go of whatever is holding you back.

Now it's time for you to try these techniques and start becoming a master of your mind!

Cue the Colors!

Master Qi wears bright colors. He's always happy! Long ago, I vowed to always wear nice colors to feel great. He inspired me to transmit the energy levels of the colors I wear even more than I already do. While I was in excruciating pain, I tried to maintain a positive attitude in all aspects of my life. If you like what you're wearing, then you're supposed to feel good, right? I realized I should wear clothes to reflect my attitude and make me feel better. Wearing specific colors would remind me of healing possibilities, of staying optimistic and hopeful. Someone once told me that dressing like this even makes your blood cells happy!

I still surround myself with the psychology of color. If you wear bright colors, your energy feeds from them. If you're down, you can bring yourself up by wearing positive and bright colors. When we get dressed we wear some colors more frequently than others. That's because we are inclined to like certain colors more. I'm attracted to like clothes on the brighter end of the spectrum. Every garment of mine looks sunny! I prefer not to wear black tops. Occasionally, I'll wear black or grey pants, but I'll balance it out with a colorful shirt and shoes.

Here's a rundown of the colors and emotions they evoke when I wear them:

Red: Energy, life forces, and my aura color, natu-
        rally! Action, will, strength, endurance, and
        power. I am very motivated when I wear red.

Orange: Empowerment, confidence, communication,
        warmth, and happiness. Wearing orange can
        be rejuvenating and makes me optimistic. I
        also feel youthful when I wear orange.

Yellow: Intellect, happiness, fun, and enthusiasm. I feel
        like I am creatively filled with new ideas when

I wear yellow. I also like wearing yellow when I need an extra boost of happiness.

Green: Growth, renewal, organization, abundance, and calmness. I feel more balanced when I wear green and have a heightened sense of vitality. An extra boost of great health, wealth, and wisdom.

Blue: Honesty, reliability, and emotional peacefulness. If I am stressed out, I wear blue to restore my sense of serenity and security.

Purple: Imagination and balance between spiritual, physical, and emotional energies. I am reminded to be even more in touch with my spirituality and I am very inspired when I wear purple.

Pink: Love, understanding, and hope. I am encouraged to express my compassion when wearing pink. I am also inspired to be hopeful about the future.

Brown: Structure, loyalty, stability, and support. I am grounded when I wear brown and feel very comfortable with whatever the day brings.

Gray: Conservative, neutral, classic. I am calmed by the color gray and wear it when I need to stay impartial.

Silver: Fluidity, equilibrium, female energy, power, dignity, and ageless wisdom. When I wear silver, I am reminded to go with the flow and remain strong.

Gold: Success, positivity, and triumph. It is an upbeat
        color that signifies victory.

To maintain my fantastic outlook on color, I never leave the house without my bright yellow jade bracelet, an emerald green ring, or my beautiful handmade green necklace with golden undertones. Definitely try implementing color in your life and you'll feel the difference!

My Apartment's Makeover

In 2015, it was renovation time in my apartment. I had an artistic vision of what my apartment should look like, and I was ready to change it up a bit. Revamping décor is always fun. The last time I renovated my apartment was many years ago. Out with the old and in with the new, upgrades are awesome!

Having a special apartment to suit my personality has always been a priority of mine. I'd definitely classify my apartment's motif as original, serene, and blissful. It's my zen zone and happy place that's decked out with framed photos, various candles, oils, crystals, and precious stones that go together so well. I wanted some softer and more relaxing lighting for my ceilings. To begin the renovations, I ripped the ugly chandelier from the ceiling and threw it away. I was glad to remove its harsh light from the room.

It's a funny story how my redecoration process continued. I was at ABC Interior looking for new lighting fixtures. I found a fixture that I didn't really like, but it was the best one there. I asked the lady behind the counter how to install it. She told me a list of instructions. A guy standing next to me who was looking at the same fixtures interjected. He said that the lady gave me incorrect information. I asked the man if he could install the fixtures for me, and he said he would. That was how I met Tom, hobbyist turned interior design extraordinaire.

Tom told me he loves interior decorating and designing. Shortly after, Tom came to my apartment. When it was time to hang the fixture, I realized I didn't like it. He said, "I'll make custom items and fixtures for your living space." I gleefully obliged and was excited to see what he would create. Tom drew plans for some customized fixtures, gathered the materials, and installed the new items to help me create a peaceful home. He made handmade light fixtures in bowls filled with chopped glass and suspended them from the ceiling with rope. It helped set the proper ambiance and eliminated unnecessary glare.

With the redecorating project at hand, I wanted to maintain the overall theme but with a few slight changes. I already had a lovely emerald green rug that lined the floor, its green shade symbolizing the color of abundance. I wanted to showcase my careful cache of rocks I'd been collecting over the years. Their colors inspire me and counterbalance the room's energy. One of my favorite installations is my wonderful Himalayan rock salt lamp that emits ions to neutralize my apartment's energy. Ultimate peace is achieved with these rocks. Honestly, I wish I had more space in my apartment so I could have rocks galore all over. To showcase my rocks, I asked Tom to make wooden shelves. Tom and I selected vintage wood to make long shelves. He also constructed a matching table, tailored to suit my apartment. Tom made the shelves and table quickly! I put my rocks right on the shelves and it all looked marvelous!

Master Qi arrived at my apartment one day to cure the feng shui and energy levels of my furniture. Feng shui is an ancient Chinese method for balancing various areas of your life. It accentuates positive energy and removes the negative, which is always necessary for your living space. Master Qi was not impressed with the positioning of a portable table and recommended for me to toss it. Before I knew it, he was carrying the table out the door, into the elevator, and outside to the curb for trash. He felt the need to remove the table because it was blocking the room's energy.

I told Master Qi that I wanted to buy a mirror to use as a tool for dance practice. He told me how a mirror would serve a greater purpose—more than just a simple decoration. It would visually expand my space, enable light to reflect around, and introduce a more productive energy flow into the room. Mirrors in rooms also bring calmness. The next day, I purchased a gigantic mirror to fill the large space on my wall behind the table. All of these changes were exciting!

I suppose you could say all of these renovations helped with my purifying process. I was so excited by all of these new changes that I could not wait for the mirror to be hung up. The next day, on Friday the 13th, the handyman arrived to hang the mirror. He had just finished, so I paid him and he walked out the door. I sat on the chair to check out the new mirror. Suddenly, the mirror came toppling down from the wall! With lightning speed, I lurched forward and sprinted over to it. I caught the mirror with my bare hands, jumping up to stop it from hitting the ground. Even though the mirror was safe and intact, the table next to me got knocked over and fell on my toe! BOOM! SMASH! At least I knew I had remarkable reflexes! I heard my toe shattering beneath me. "Yow!" I screamed. My big toe was in agony. It felt like someone had shot me in the toe. I almost passed out from the pain. I needed to seek immediate medical attention! I could not believe what had just happened; it was surreal, and I could not fathom that I was injured yet again. I'm not at all superstitious, but this event occurring on Friday the 13th was very bizarre! And the mirror stayed fully intact!

During my hospital visit, I found out that I had broken my toe, shattering it in over 20 places. I had to wear this absurd rocket boot. It looked like I was blasting off into space and ready for a walk on the moon. I came back home from the hospital and got some rest. Resting is always difficult for me because I love being active; however, rest was what my body craved and needed.

The next morning, I was in anguish! I stayed home from work to rest and elevate my leg, keeping the pressure off my toe. There had to be some good from this crazy accident...

I went back to the doctor the following week for a checkup. My toe was unwrapped and it was so swollen! At least there was oxygen flowing into it. Proper breathing, meditation, and yoga saved the life of my toe. If the mirror fell on my toe six years earlier, I would have lost it. Back then, I couldn't even feel or wiggle my toes because blood and oxygen weren't reaching my feet properly. Now, I can do more than that! I'm breathing properly, getting my blood flowing all over my body, and took preventative measures by all of the healing practice I had been doing. I am so grateful for the work I did to pre-empt future problems. YAY!

I had an epiphany about what this whole event truly meant. It finally occurred to me that I had to take this incident as a sign to relax and pay attention to details. I realized that the mirror falling represented my need to refocus my priorities. I needed more time to myself. Through my toes, I needed to focus on re-grounding. This event was telling me to slow down and take more time for intro-spection and self-examination. Saying that I was burning the candle at both ends would have been the understatement of the century. Between work, activism, and my family life, I was running around, launching myself on unwavering missions, and not truly taking time to unwind!

The mirror falling on me was a symbol. I recognized that mir-rors, in and of themselves, represent self-love and awareness. In the Greek oracle of Apollo at Delphi, the mirror is stated as "knowing thyself," to represent higher understanding and perception at all ends of the spectrum. For mirrors to display a reflection, you need light. This light denotes wisdom, cognizance, and illumination. Mirrors also have the same effect as water, allowing your thoughts to toss about on the ocean and contemplate life as you know it to be.

The combination of mirrors and light can literally mean that I needed to take a deeper look within myself and take time for spir-itual and emotional reflection. I had to evaluate my current under-standings of things through the lens of enlightenment.

When I look in the mirror, I see my eyes are windows to the soul, displaying my most inward emotions. It is within my power to call upon myself and ponder metaphysical questions that make up my existence. I embrace the reflection staring back at me because I have a great self-esteem. I have a beautiful soul, inside and out. Just as the mirror shows what is physically there on the surface and what is present in the world around me, the mirror also encourages me to ponder deeper matters. It also represents how I appear to the outside world, and to what extent my internal musings are reflected and expressed outwardly. What I needed to further work on was eliminating toxins that still harbored within.

In addition to these physical wounds, I was still recovering from these emotional injuries, and now would be a great time to reflect and take my much needed "me" time. I had accepted that my special month was officially beginning.

Fast forwarding three weeks later, I was unpacking from a trip. I moved my suitcase slightly, and my laptop catapulted from my bag and fell on that same toe. I was again in pain! I collapsed on the bed and cried. I was completely crippled!

A week after this incident, I was catching up on emails at my desk, and suddenly, my favorite analog clock came tumbling down from the wall. I was astounded! That clock had been on the wall for years! This had to be another sign! When thinking about this event later on, I realized that the clock falling from the wall was a divine omen to clarify the meaning of the falling mirror. It was time to seek more clarity in life, gradually slower my pace, and just breathe.

After all of this, my room renovations were complete! The mirror had found its final resting spot on my wall. The clock was mounted back up in its spot. But I had some additional thinking to do. With a broken toe and reflective mind, the next chapter of my healing had unfolded before me.

I was still making progress with dance lessons, focusing on taking it easy. These lessons were like therapy! Hip shaking here, shimmying there, and clapping out awesome rhythms in dance—I was having the time of my life. Even with the broken toe, I was still dancing with other parts of my body! I was taught different stretches and isolations to stay in tune with the unbelievable progress I made. I would enthusiastically participate in clapping and drumming sessions, where I'd learn rhythmic wisdom.

Two weeks after the repeat toe incident, I woke up with horrendous shoulder pain. Strange tingling went down my arm. I was in so much pain. I thought I was back to square one, stage one of my injuries. When I pushed my hand up to the mirror as it fell, my arms reached to catch it and I pulled my neck out. This was the start of another injury! Then during isolations in dance with Cecilia, I accidentally strained my neck, stretching it too far and pushing my body too hard. I was having such a blast on the dance floor that I did not realize how I was actually suffering from overexertion.

It was a holiday weekend, so I wanted to enjoy time with my family by overlooking the pain. Besides, I knew my primary doctor would be closed for business that weekend. Can you guess who I called after the holiday weekend? That's right—I phoned my hero, Dr. Kerr! He said, "Why didn't you call me as soon as you were in pain? I would've seen you over the weekend!" You see what I mean? He's hero material: always ready, anytime, anywhere, to help me with my injuries!

It was time for another session Kerr-tastic session early Monday morning. He determined I was suffering from overexertion in the shoulder and neck. Dr. Kerr advised, "Debbie, you've got to take it easy!" He told me to stop dancing until I recovered (which I begrudgingly obliged, of course). I needed to stop pushing myself and just chill for once.

The Month of Me and Meditation

All of these events led me to deem April 2015 the "Month of Me and Meditation." Keeping my injuries in mind, I allotted time for activities like meditation, solace, and relaxation each day.

Yoga is a form of full body meditation that I had become accustomed to, but in my practically crippled state, I needed to do more sedentary activities. I wanted to practice more stationary tranquility. I'd practiced meditation on and off in the past, but now it was time to get down to business on the meditative side of things. I knew that it was all about clearing the mind and focusing on the breath.

I started to seriously meditate in my room by sitting down, trying to favor my broken toe. I faced the balcony, adjusted my posture, and took a deep breath to start my meditation session. I used visualization to calm down my mind. I closed my eyes and entered a meditative state. With the power of my imagination, I pictured a waterfall alongside a lush seaside forest. That first session lasted no longer than five minutes. I thought to myself, "Is my mind too active for meditation?" I had to put mind over matter. At first, I couldn't bring myself to sit quietly and clear my mind. This was because I was focusing on a million different things at once! I kept thinking about my painful toe, my shoulder, and other things going on in my life. After all, that's what red aura individuals specialize in—thinking about what's next on the docket called life! Now, I've learned to overlook my active mind during meditation and put it on pause for a chunk of time each day. I started meditating for five-minute increments and now have worked my way up to 30 minutes at a time.

Master Qi always told me that meditation would work wonders. In fact, meditation is how Master Qi achieves his high level of energy. He reiterated, "Debbie, you've got to meditate!" I thought his obsession with meditation was crazy, because it was such a simple tactic. I kept complaining about my hot flashes and other bodily issues, and his answer was, "MEDITATE!" We went back and forth for about 10 emails, and finally it sunk in. "I just *have* to meditate," I thought to myself. It was that easy. This reconfirmed the simplicity of life for me.

For me, meditating takes me on a "staycation" away from my current mindset. These times are luxurious. I had to find the spot that I was visualizing in my original indoor meditation sessions. Because the weather was lovely in spring 2015, I found a beautiful spot close to the water on FDR Drive for meditation practice. The water has such healing and restorative powers, enabling me to feel better. My outdoor sessions are always gratifying! During meditation coaching with Master Qi, we've meditated outside together too!

My meditation progress has advanced quite nicely. Now when I meditate, I imagine myself sitting under the waterfall with cascading water running over my body, through my head and out over my toes, flushing out toxins that have harbored in my body. I really started to filter the airflow rushing even faster through my body. It is so empowering, embodying energy manifestation.

I've trained myself to meditate for long periods of time, and I view meditation as a joyfully rewarding experience. I look forward to my meditative state each day. Now that my body is so conditioned to this regimen, I feel discombobulated if I happen to skip a day. For example, one day, my schedule didn't allow me to meditate. I ran from work to dinner, resulting in a bout of hot flashes. I knew that this happened because I skipped my meditation! The next day, I made sure to have ample meditation time to make up for the previous day's snafu. I had no hot flashes! Since I've started meditating seriously, my hot flashes have lessened and I have peace of mind. It just goes to show how powerful meditation is!

Fast forward to a few months after my initial meditations… I went to go visit my parents for a weekend and it felt like I was on vacation. I sat in a luxurious pool under the cascading waterfall, closed my eyes, and just meditated. I was so relaxed!! As the water flowed over my head, I metaphorically felt the toxins rush out of my body and float away with the tide—for real this time. I was officially at peace. It was one of the most surreal feelings ever. In that moment, one of the most definitive bricks in my house's healing foundation had been placed.

I realized how meditation can really help me and wanted to try flotation therapy—a practice where you float in a salt bath to detox and chill. I was so excited to relax when submerged in the luxurious comfort contained in a tub of water. I found NYC's La Casa Spa and Wellness Center, which looked like the ideal place for my flotation journey to begin! I liked its mantra, specializing in "holistic wellness and natural cleansing." Totally my type of place!

Invented in the 1950s, flotation therapy has transformational effects that have many healing results on the body. It is the equivalent of five solid hours of sleep. The body interprets this treatment as a three-day fast and starts the process of detoxification. Epsom salt is added to the water to increase its density and release its healing powers. Flotation stimulates the body into a state of rest and this process has many physiological effects on the body. Research has shown that floatation slows your pulse, lowers blood pressure, increases blood circulation, increases alpha/theta brainwave activity, and allows heavy metal detoxification to occur in the body. It also re-mineralizes the skin, improves skin's elasticity, and allows the body to decrease its release of stress hormones to calm you down.

It was my turn to try this treatment out. I walked into the tranquil flotation room. As I entered the salty tub and floated in a warm bath of mineralized salts, I felt like I was hovering in the clouds. The serene consciousness I entered was meditative and enabled me to reflect and rejuvenate. Sure, I could soak in my own bathtub, but this type of flotation is much different. In an official flotation bath, moisture is removed from the skin and the bath's salt gets stored in the uppermost layer of your skin. It binds the water within your skin to maintain its elasticity and hydrate your outer protective layers. After the bath, you'll have less dry skin and feel renewed. Flotation was a nice supplement to my detoxification process. My emotional, physical, and spiritual states of wellbeing were reinforced. La Casa Day Spa is really great because it's an all-in-one place! They also do colonics, massages, magnetic pulse therapy, energy healing, facials, and body wraps.

Starting with seated meditation in my home, to walking meditation with Master Qi, floating meditation really sealed the deal. My friends go to the gym for hours, pumping iron and having intense cardio sessions to de-stress. I was once one of those people, a gym fanatic who thought intense workouts were everything. But now, I have realized that things are much simpler than that. Meditation is quite contrary to what used to be my daily routine. The old adage, "Whatever floats your boat" is accurate. These new and improved daily healing processes now float my boat further and pave for even smoother sailing. You can achieve enhanced states of mind and life through meditation, simplicity, and relaxation. It really can't get any better than this. Sailing on toward the sunset of success, you have it made.

I am on my way to feeling 100% wonderful every day, getting better and better all the time! I am simultaneously calm, cool, collected, and energetic. My health plan is promoting energy production in cells, releasing tension through breathing, actively seeking physical freedom, and becoming mellower through each new day. And I feel that my healing process is coming full circle.

CHAPTER 17:

My Favorite Foods Are the Cherries on Top

No healing process is complete without a balanced diet! The dishes that I eat are so delicious, and I pride myself on eating well. My diet mainly consists of raw foods and fish, where most of what I eat isn't genetically engineered. And everything is still tasty! Veggies are my favorite! Eating food in its most natural state gives your body the essential vitamins and enzymes it needs to function properly. Raw foodists have exercised these principles for centuries. This dietary practice stresses that when food is cooked higher than 120°F, all nutritional value is lost. When cooked, foods such as broccoli lose all cancer-fighting properties. Essential vitamins like vitamin C and folic acid evaporate into thin air when prepared. This is why I opt for healthier, raw food.

When shopping for food, I try to avoid products containing GMOs. I was horrified to learn about GMOs and how most veggies contain them. GMOs are "genetically modified organisms": entities in which the natural makeup has been changed via genetic engineering technology. With these procedures, genetic modification occurs. This means that it is being altered from its natural state by the addition, deletion, or mutation of the food's genes. With GMOs, the food becomes more synthetic and tainted. Just the thought of GMOs makes me sick! To me, eating GMOs is like ingesting fake food! I am so passionate about getting rid of GMOs in America that I am in the process of protesting them. I always look for the "Non-GMO Project Verified.org" stamp to affirm that the product doesn't contain GMOs.

Food is supposed to energize you, not weigh you down and turn you into a sloth. If I choose to indulge from time to time on unhealthy choices, I brace myself for the consequence of feeling ill from food. Now, when faced with options to break my healthy eating, I have no desire to eat junk. It is a vicious cycle: the more you eat of a food, the more your body wants it. When you're changing your eating habits, you'll probably feel like a drug addict going through withdrawal symptoms. It takes the average person 21 days to form a habit. If you're planning on changing your diet, you'll be fine after the 21-day hurdle! You'll start craving junk food less and less until you no longer want it at all!

My diet is energizing and I look younger from my healthy meals. Eating cleaner can even decrease potential risk of disease. When you consume fewer trans and saturated fats, lower your sugar intake, and decrease sodium intake, your body will digest the food better and absorb more necessary nutrients. Unhealthy eating slows your body down and does not enable it to function at its maximum capacity.

Are you curious what my daily food plan is like? Here's what I eat: I usually start my day with a berry drink, and then I'll have a sprout drink later on. Lunch is often a super food like quinoa, accompanied with an arugula salad. For dinner, I like to have wild fish with a green salad four times a week. I look forward to my special drinks every day because they give me an instant energy boost! They help me feel fuller longer because of all of the protein in the sprouts. It's loaded with fiber, which helps anyone lose weight. Healthy drinks can lower your blood pressure, lower your cholesterol, boost calcium intake, and promote bone health.

Are you inspired to get on board with healthy eating? Check out some of my favorite recipes to get you jumpstarted on a clean-eating, healthy-living kick. Bon appétit!

Energizing Green Drink:

1 handful of raw nuts (soaked)

1 lb. sunflower sprouts from Perfect Foods (800-933-3288)

10 oz. coconut water

2 figs (optional)

Cinnamon, cayenne pepper, or apple (also optional)

Let the almonds soak overnight. This helps release the vital nutrients and enables your body to digest the nuts more easily. Drain the water and put all ingredients in the blender. Add the sunflower sprouts to the coconut water and blend. If the drink is still too thick, add more coconut water or distilled water.

Very Berry Smoothie:

2 cups coconut milk

1 teaspoon coconut oil

1 cup raspberries

½ cup non-GMO granola or soaked almonds

½ cup blueberries

1 cup strawberries

½ cup blackberries

1 piece ginger (to help with inflammation in the body)

1 banana or mango or papaya (optional)

Pop all these ingredients in the blender and mix! If the consistency is too thick, just add more coconut milk. I concoct this drink and the one below every morning and take them with me to work.

Liquid Gold Juice:

2 green apples

4 stalks celery (remove the leaves)

1 cucumber

6 kale leaves

½ lemon

1 inch ginger

Cut every ingredient into small pieces, add to the blender, pour, and enjoy!

Power peanut butter and berry protein smoothie:

1 frozen banana

1 cup frozen blueberries

1 tablespoon peanut butter

1 teaspoon protein powder, plant-based or whey powder

Place all ingredients in the blender and blend until desired consistency is reached. Add ice if you wish!

Raw Italian-style pesto pasta:

You can use a spiralizer for this recipe
Pasta:
Either 1 squash or 1 zucchini
1 large tomato, sliced

Pesto:
1 bunch basil leaves
3 tablespoons olive oil
1 cup oregano leaves
1 cup walnuts
2 garlic cloves
½ teaspoon salt
3 tablespoons water
1 crushed tomato for sauce

"Pasta": Slice either the squash or zucchini into spaghetti-like strands. For the pesto, combine all ingredients into a food processor and pulse until it becomes a paste. When finished, serve the pesto on top of the pasta, and add sliced tomatoes as garnish.

Cauliflower crust pizza:

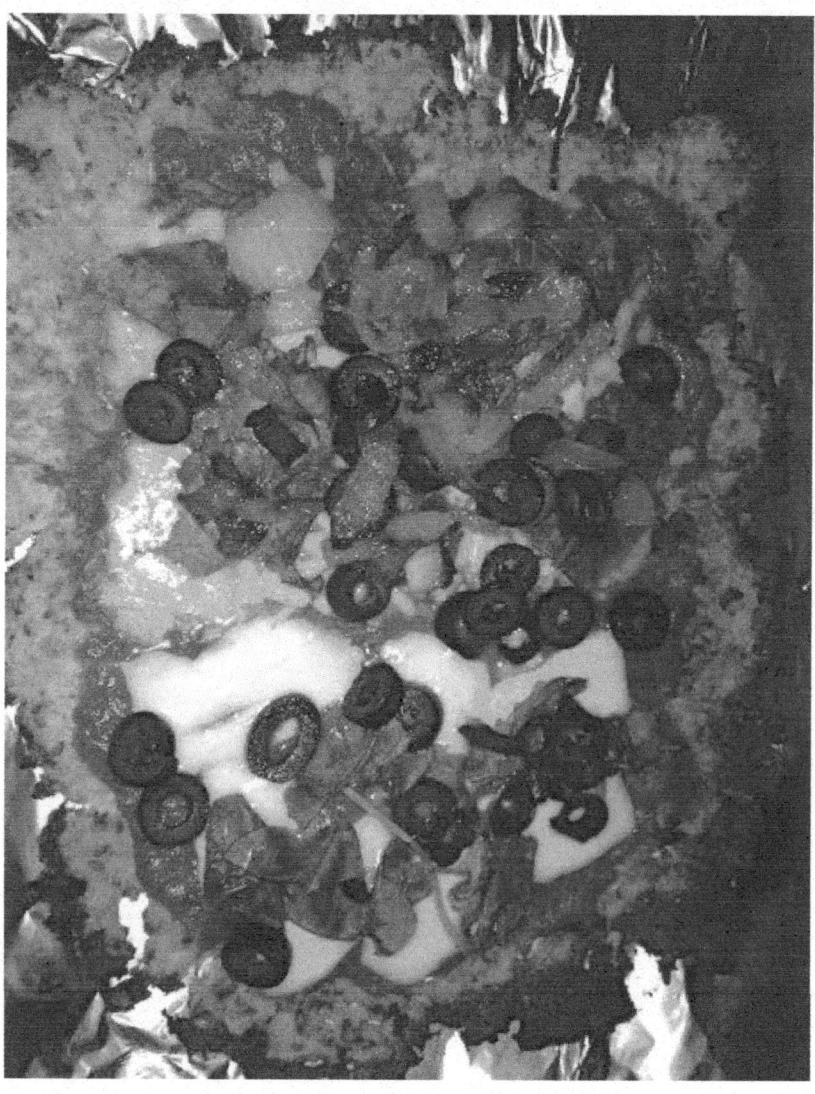

Ingredients:

2 heads cauliflower

¼ teaspoon oregano

1 tablespoon garlic powder

¼ teaspoon salt

6 tablespoons flax seeds

½ **cup** almond meal

Any pizza toppings and cheese of your choice!

****Ingredients tailored for personal taste and appetite****

Steam the cauliflower. In a bowl, grind the cauliflower into a pulp-like consistency. Add the oregano, garlic powder, flax seeds, and almond meal. Mix into a dough-like consistency. Grease the baking sheet with cooking spray or oil (I like coconut oil). Place the dough on a baking sheet and flatten it. Bake it in the oven for one hour on 400 degrees F. Take the pan out and flip over the pizza. Cook the other side for one hour on 400 degrees. After it's baked to perfection, take the cauli-dough out of the oven and add whatever toppings you like! I like to add crushed tomatoes, olives, and veggies!

Lentil Hummus Burger:

Ingredients for 8 burgers:
1 cup sprouted lentils (soak for 30 minutes beforehand)
2 tablespoons chia seeds
¼ cup fresh basil
¼ cup and 2 tablespoons hummus
3 tablespoons nutritional yeast
½ teaspoon salt

Put all ingredients, except the chia seeds, into the food processor. Pulse thoroughly. Add the chia seeds and pulse until everything sticks together. Remove the contents from the food processor and shape into the shape of a burger. Put the burgers into a dehydrator and dehydrate at 105°F for two hours. If you don't have a dehydrator or want to cook it in an oven, cook at 350°F for 20 minutes.

Kale salad with chickpeas and tempeh:

It's a power bowl because it's super-packed with protein!

Ingredients:
2 oz. tempeh (raw or sautéed with sesame oil)
¼ lb. chopped kale
½ can chickpeas
Shredded carrots
2 tablespoons sesame seeds

Add everything to a bowl, add dressing as desired (I recommend oil and vinegar), and enjoy!

You can add cashew cream to this recipe for extra protein!
Cashew cream:
1 cup cashews (soaked in water for four hours)

11 tablespoons water

2-3 tablespoons lemon juice

Once soaked, wash the cashews, add the water and lemon juice, and pulse in a food processor. After you've followed all these steps, assemble the salad in a bowl.

Raw vegan fudge tarts (my sister's specialty):

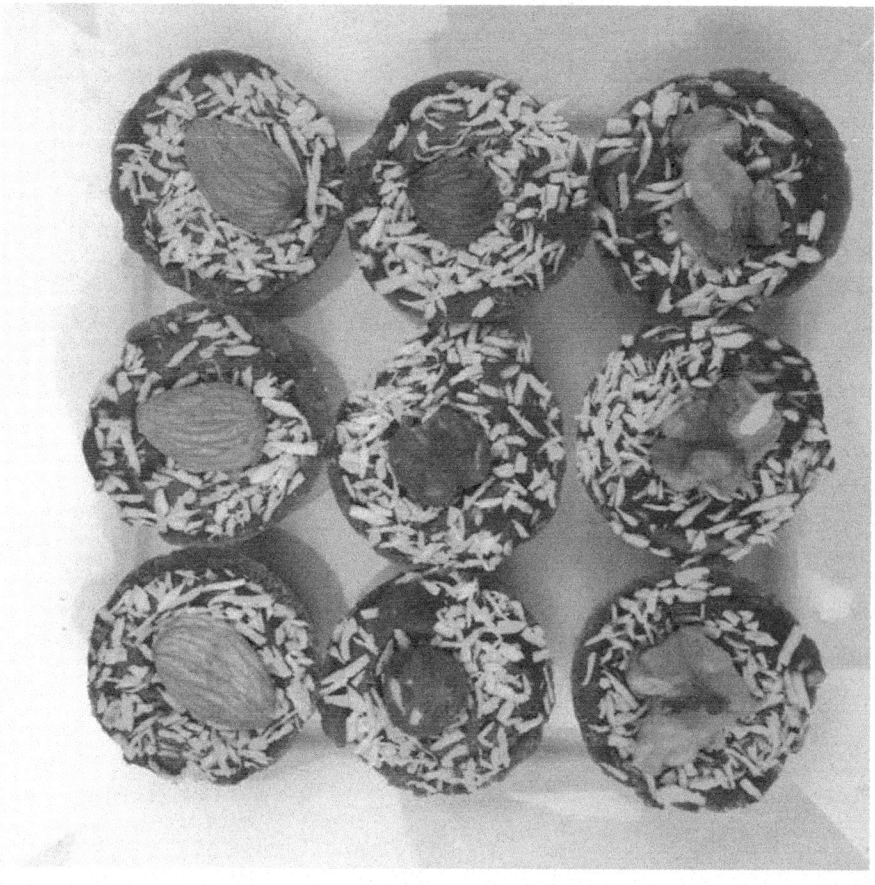

For the tart crust:

¾ cup cocoa nibs

1 cup almond flour

½ cup maple syrup powder

¼ cup maple syrup

¼ cup coconut oil

¼ cup coconut butter

Blend in a food processor to get it to stick together. You might have to add more coconut butter.

For the inside:

2 ¼ cup cocoa power

2 ½ cups maple syrup

1 cup coconut butter (should be creamy)

Top with nuts or coconut flakes

Put the filler inside the tart crust and enjoy!

CHAPTER 18:

My Italian Adventure

Despite my toe injury, I went on an excursion to Italy in summer 2015. I was looking forward to having lots of "me" time in a lovely town. I arrived in Taormina, Italy, and accidently gave the wrong Airbnb address to the taxi driver. But I did not realize this was happening until after I arrived at the wrong place. I exited the cab and knocked on the door. An old lady who greeted me like a long-lost cousin escorted my luggage and me into the residence. She did not speak any English. She showed me to my room and it was totally rundown. It didn't look like the photo on Airbnb and everything was very depressing. After I showered, I went to grab food, and wanted to figure out if I should leave this room because I didn't like it.

Suddenly, the people who I actually rented the Airbnb place from texted me and said their mother was waiting for me at the house. I told them I already met their mother. They said I hadn't arrived there yet. I said, "But I'm right here!" Then, I realized I was at the wrong house! I was thankful that I trusted in the process of what was happening, packed up my stuff, left that room, and safely made it to the real Airbnb place I originally booked. Can you believe this actually happened? You cannot make this stuff up!

Throughout my trip, I took great care of my body and ate delicious meals. My favorite meal was at a luxurious five-star hotel facing the ocean in Taormina. There I noshed on the branzino fish lunch and had lush greens. I always ate a balanced plate brimming with healthy foods.

I took a boat tour through Taormina's Blue Cave while staying by the seaside. The water was a vibrant shade of blue. It was picturesque! Italy is one of my favorite countries to visit because it's so beautiful! I admired the rocky caverns and was amazed by the hanging stalactites inside the cave, which have great energy. This trip was definitely part of my healing process.

In Sicily's Alcantara Falls, I saw people body rafting down the river. I thought to myself, "That looks like so much fun! I love trying new things." I watched some people on the swerving path going down the designated body rafting area. I had to try it! It's like white water rafting but without the raft and rocks. I even tried to get some of my new friends I made on my trip go with me, but they thought it was an absurd idea. They were like, "Debbie, are you out of your mind?" I said, "I need to try this. It looks great!"

I put on a wetsuit and helmet and started sliding down the incline over sharp rocks and fast drops. The instructor told me to float down the river and keep my knees bent. After the first winding turn down the path, I got a bad gut feeling about my body rafting ride. I was getting nervous. I hit the bottom of my feet against the rocks with great velocity because I was going so fast. I got out of the danger zone and enjoyed getting safely to land. I couldn't deal with it. The impact was not good! I didn't think anything of it, but the following morning, my ankle and toe were killing me.

The fact that I even decided to go body rafting after my broken toe and other injuries is mind boggling. I learned how I couldn't do crazy things like this! I am a fine flower. I can't risk getting injured in reckless ways like body rafting! I always need to take my health and safety into consideration before doing *anything*. How ridiculous does body rafting sound now? Never will I do that again!

After feeling better, I visited Ravello's scenic Villa Cimbrone that overlooks the ocean. I climbed the trails and enjoyed nature.

While walking in the woods, I took many photos. I turned around from photographing the foliage and saw a staircase, symbolizing the step-by-step path of healing I'd been on. I knew that I needed to photograph it. That would be my cover photo for *Happy Healing!* The photo came out beautifully!

I was at a beach in Elba Islands that was super rocky. The water was crystal clear and so warm! Swimming in Italian water was like a form of rebirth all over again! I took a break from swimming to relax on a floating beach mat. I was nearly falling asleep when the hat I was holding flew from my hand in the wind. The water's current was carrying the hat away. I jumped up from the floating beach mat to get the hat and smashed my bad toe on a rock. "Yowwwwwww!" I screamed.

Later when I was ready to leave, I had to walk up the beach's hill to the taxi in the blaring heat. When I arrived back in my room, I elevated my leg to take the pressure off my toe, praying for my pain to vanish in the morning. I wrapped my toe in bandages for extra support. I was scared when I was in bed. I was in agony from my toe. It was now midnight. That's when I got a text from Master Qi! It said, "Debra, are you okay?" I went "Holy shit!" He felt my pain. He knew I'd injured my toe during that silly beach episode. He texted me back and said that my toe would be healed soon.

I went to sleep that night with a very sore toe and thought about just how fragile I was. In the morning I felt healed and energized. "Where was this feeling coming from?" I thought to myself. My toe didn't hurt anymore. I peeled off my toe's wrapping and the swelling had gone down too! I realized that Master Qi had sent me energy across the ocean from many miles away. I was so excited by this. I had been healed by his energy again!

During my trip, I also went to Ponza and climbed Mt. Etna. Here are several of my favorite photos from the trip.

Elba Islands in Tuscany, Italy

Elba Islands

While I was completing my final draft of *Happy Healing*, I did Tarot card and tea leaf readings. I like to consult these every once in a while to see what they have to tell me.

For my tea leaf reading, I put my energy on the cup, sloshed the glass, and asked what the universe had in store for me. After pouring out the water, the cup revealed many images: a swimmer doing laps in water, a bird soaring with outstretched wings, and a heart! I consulted a tea leaf reading dictionary to decipher the meanings. The swimmer represents overcoming fears and obstacles while reaching goals and staying afloat. The flying bird means communication, news, and motion. The heart is an omen, being expansive to love, foretelling exciting events on the horizon.

My 10-card Tarot spread was an eclectic combination of cards. For my ideal card in the reading, I received the King of Pentacles. This card shows a regal man sitting atop a throne with a golden scepter in one hand and a pentacle in the other. It signifies all elements present in the human world: earth, air, fire, and water. The king on the card is pictured with flowers, plants, a ram's head, and fruit that signify abundance. In the card's background, there is a castle to symbolize fortitude and grand efforts to attain goals. The symbols on the King of Pentacles card represent accomplishment. Just like the King of Pentacles, I have achieved my healing goals. And there is still more goodness to come in the future.

My readings reaffirmed the true trail I'm meant to be on and encouraged me to do everything in my willpower to make it work! I have taken the best possible journey. I have all the skills and tools to move forward in life. I'm on the right track and trust in the universe 100%.

In October 2015, I was scared for my life because my blood pressure suddenly skyrocketed. When I start to worry, my blood pressure goes through the roof. My blood pressure is directly related to my emotions. When I returned from the expo, I worried about different things that were going on in my life. This worrying became a huge stressor, taking a toll on my body. My heart and mind simultaneously started racing. I was trembling from head to toe. My blood pressure went from 198 all the way up to 215. I was about to go to the hospital when I realized I needed to calm my mind, stop the mush-mosh I was creating for myself, and meditate. Even if I did go to the hospital, I would be given medication that wouldn't work anyway. I always had an adverse reaction to pills. Also, pills for high blood pressure do not control your emotions; they just lower the number of your blood pressure reading and do not get to the root of the problem. I was getting so nervous because my blood pressure wasn't getting lower.

That night, I called Master Qi at 11:30 p.m., and he said, "Debbie, you've got to sit quietly, focus on meditating and creating positive energy. I will pray for you and send you healing energy." Once again, he saved my life by encouraging me to simply meditate. I put my feet up, concentrated on breathing, relaxed in bed, and held happy thoughts. I pictured myself floating in a red bikini underneath a waterfall, kicking in the water, the ocean ahead of me, with blue skies overhead, and trees surrounding the area. I then pictured myself playing on a swing set, just like I did when I was little, swinging back and forth, enjoying the moment. I concentrated on my inner child and got back to my youthful nature to heal my mind and body; this is what qi-energy healing and meditation are all about, enabling you to channel your inner vitality. Feeling like a child, without any inhibitions, feeling limitless and boundless, always calms me down.

By 1:00 a.m., the wee hours after my scary aforementioned incident, my blood pressure went back down to 156 with meditation and relaxation, allowing me to heal. Meditation and Master Qi's prayers saved my life!

In addition, I've come up with my own strategies to calm myself down, let my worries vanish into thin air, and keep my blood pressure down. The thoughts in our own heads, which we create, can make us sick. We need to filter what we think about, be upbeat at all times, and meditate to dispel these thoughts by generating our own positivity. Remember, you are always in control of your own happiness. You cannot place your happiness in the hands of others, hoping they will make you content. It is your responsibility to find your own bliss and do what makes you happy at all times. Do not compromise your happiness to please others, and don't let others stress you out! Master Qi once sent me this cartoon. I agree with this wholeheartedly:

I love to focus on constructive visualizations and keep an optimistic outlook. If I do feel stressed out, I try the following strategies: When I walk down the street, I maintain my confidence with a youthful mindset. I picture myself walking down the street with a crown over my head (since I was a queen in past lives, and still am a queen in my own mindset today)! While I walk, I imagine a waterfall flowing over my head to calm my mind and worries. This targets how I lower my blood pressure and monitor my own emotions. I am in charge of my destiny, and monitoring my blood pressure weekly with my portable BP cuff is so important; it is a life-or-death health situation for me. So, I enthusiastically continue onward.

The day after this blood pressure incident, I started my next health mission at the NewLife Expo in 2015. This yearly expo focuses on health and wellness, bringing many like-minded people together in NYC for a weekend in October. Be sure to check it out next October if you'll be in NYC. Of course, I looked forward to seeing Master Qi, and I was excited to meet new healers. I couldn't wait to scour the tents and have more exhilarating healing experiences.

I walked around the tents and found the singing bowl section. Here is where I tried singing bowls for the first time. Singing bowls are a type of bell that can be placed on a surface, like a table, and then played. You can manipulate the bowls to produce sounds. Singing bowls help you relax, meditate, maintain your health, and have fun with music! They can be found around the world in places of meditation and love, like Buddhist temples. In different countries the sound of bowls can be used with chanting, meditating, or to mark that practice is in session. Anyone can start playing them easily!

I was drawn to the expo's singing bowl booth right away because that area was emanating such great energy. The bowls made nice sounds and I wanted to learn how to do it! When I went over to that special table, the person at the booth instructed me how to make the bowls sing. He handed me a leather-wrapped mallet and told me to strike the rim of the bowl. I experimented with this technique and also swooped the mallet around the bowl's rim in a circular motion. When I did this, the bowl started producing harmonic tones and sang to me! Naturally, my instinct was to sing along with the bowl. I knew that this technique unleashed something special inside, something that made me feel like a child—I wanted to sing! Paul said that singing bowls enable us to honor our inner child, hence making us feel youthful. Without any inhibitions, I became my own chorus, sang a lovely melody, and had a wonderful time! I highly recommend trying singing bowls!

The Beat Goes On...

All of this has truly been life's work, a mission that I have been so proud to broadcast to the world. When I was in the final drafting stages of this book, I had yet to decide on a title. I asked the universe to assist me with the final touches and bestow me with the perfect inspiration for a title. I rode in a cab to work one morning and contemplated this. As I entered the cab, the 75-year-old driver cheerfully greeted me with a striking level of energy. She expressed interest in the rocker boot I wore for my toe. On the ride to work, I gave her a brief rundown of what I'd been going through with my injuries and overall healing process so far.

By telling my story to a stranger, sitting in a random cab, I was open to receive the universe's offerings. It would deliver what I was looking for and help me polish the final touches of my book.

As I exited the cab, the driver exclaimed, "Happy Healing! And pay attention to details!" I thought to myself that, yes, I have been on the path of happy healing. I am still extremely content with the route of wellness I have chosen. And just like the events surrounding the mirror incident, I need to pay attention to details.

This encounter with the cab driver was serendipitous and so opportune! She had inspired me to make *Happy Healing* the title of my book! This occurrence just confirms the universe's special way of working. When you embrace the unknown and ask the universe, you will receive blessings. Comparably to the time when I saw the message via the car's license plate in the tunnel (when the car cut me off and told me to pursue life insurance), this message for the book's title came at a time when I least expected it and when I needed it the most. This cab driver was like a guardian angel helping me along the way. I am a part of all that I have met.

Through my journey, I've been learning so many lifelong lessons. I realized that I still think out-of-the-box, embrace all, find great solutions, trust in the process, and always maintain a positive attitude. Me, I'm one of the most happy-go-lucky people you'll ever meet. With this outlook, every day is the best day ever and I'm always ready for the next adventure. From the moment I wake up, the air smells sweeter, the sky shines brighter, and I am incredibly happy.

I am freer in all meanings of the word—emotionally, physically, and spiritually. I feel like a new person who is healthy, humbled, wise, and ready to take on the world! In fact, I feel like through this journey, I became my own personal superhero, complete with a cape of self-wisdom and strength!

With all I have been through, I did not wallow in my self-pity because that would not have been productive. I was proactive, rather than reactive, and I found solutions to cure each of my issues. My curious nature, desperation, and willingness to heal forced me to face my trials and tribulations and be ready to take on the lifelong mission of being the best possible version of Debra Betesh that I could possibly be.

I am now even more appreciative of each blessing that has been bestowed upon me. All is good and grand. I believe that everything happens for a reason, and we are presented with exactly what we can handle. Working with the unforeseen, with what we can and cannot control, we must defeat the inner issues that lie within to move forward in life and learn in the process.

I embrace life as it comes at me, and I face my fears. I've learned that everything can be simplified down to its smallest means to make life more manageable. We make life more complicated than it really has to be. This is a product of the mind's attempt to cope with circumstances and defense mechanisms for life's encounters.

But things don't have to be this difficult! Improving your mental skills will make all the difference. It's all in the mind, so overthrow your self-defeating mindset, be kind to yourself, and things will be easier. When you accept the unknown and life's simplicity, the universe opens up to you on a whole other level. This also enables you to remove the blockages you have constructed. Once we eliminate the drama from our lives and get back to basics, everything is simple and we have it made.

Today, I continue on the journey of healing and have a great daily regimen that works wonders for me. I do Master Qi's dances in the morning and at night. I also meditate in the morning and at night. Sometimes I sit and meditate, sometimes I move around to keep the energy positively flowing through my psyche and air moving in my body—it surpasses my lofty expectations for healing. I love listening to Chinese meditation music. My body has been revitalized, my red aura's color has brightened, and I continue to feel great. As part of my routine, Master Qi encouraged me to scrub my face and hands with Tom's toothpaste for maximum skin exfoliation. It got rid of the wrinkles that once lined my hands! He also advised me to boil banana peels and soak my feet in the infused water. I also do 30 minutes of yoga toes, where I insert a toe separator, wiggle my toes, and breathe energy into that area. I also practice oil pulling, where I put a spoon of coconut oil in my mouth for 15 minutes every morning, and then spit it out. I'll occasionally roll a ball on the bottom of my feet and stretch them for top foot performance.

Just like my simple daily routine, life is all about the choices we make and the work we do to meet our own personal goals. You need to visualize what you want to happen to make it a reality. Make it your mission to get where you want to be and carve the way to get there through a process of happiness, health, abundance, and well-being. I treat myself like gold. I am a beautiful, delicate flower that keeps blossoming more and more beautifully each year. I must be kind to myself, keep safe, and be careful. My healing tree has attained its lush green state, with lovely branches that have sprouted along my journey, catalyzed by my healing where I am firmly supported and rooted.

YES you can, and you will! Today is the day to get on the right path, and be the best possible you. I did it, and now it's time for you to plant your healing seeds, put your best foot forward, and do it too! On you grow! Stay tuned for more healing adventures as I embark on more international excursions in the coming years.

Disclaimer: *Happy Healing* **was written for informational, motivational, and entertainment purposes. It is solely Debra Betesh's experience. It is not intended as professional advice. This book should not be used to treat or diagnose any medical condition. For diagnosis or treatment of any medical problem, consult a physician. The publisher and author are not responsible for any specific health or allergic reactions that may require medical supervision or attention and are not liable for any damages or negative consequences from any treatment, action, application, or preparation to any person reading or following the information in this book. The content of this book is the author's expression on this subject matter. Individuals are solely responsible for their own choices, actions, and results.**

ACKNOWLEDGMENTS:

A heartfelt thanks to the many people who helped me with this book! I'd like to thank the fabulous B. Smoak, for her creativity, helpfulness, and zeal. With the organizational support from my edit team, my book was complete! To my wonderful healers who helped me along the way, grazie mille! The healers were key to my process because they believed healing was possible. I thank them for their support and coaching! I couldn't have done it without them! I am grateful for my parents. They inspire me to move forward and always do my best! And to my sisters and children, I am glad you all challenged me to take the holistic path of healing. Lastly, I would like to commend my body for being strong while allowing me to take the road to recovery.

List of healers in order of appearance:

Ray Pergola
raypergola@aol.com
massage therapist

Dr. Kerr
Atlas Orthogonal NYC
www.drkerr.net

Kate Hildebrandt
Structural Integration of Chelsea
www.structuralintegrationofchelsea.com

Dr. Tatz
www.nyphysicaltherapist.com

Henri Velandia
dance instructor
www.zenzouk.com

Anne-Marie Duchêne
art of alignment
www.artofalignment.com

Bassam Younes
rebirthing
www.facebook.com/BassamYounesSpiritualintuitive

Yoga with Lola Rephann
www.dakinisbliss.wordpress.com/about

Bill Hedberg
Shen Tao Studio
www.shentaostudio.com

Stem Cell of America
www.stemcellofamerica.com

Cecilia Marta
the "Rhythm Queen"
www.ceciliamarta.com

Landmark
www.landmarkworldwide.com

Master Qi Feilong
www.shaolinworld.com

La Casa Spa and Wellness Center
www.lacasaspa.com

The Morrison Center
www.morrisonhealth.com